THE REAL PALESTINIAN PROBLEM IS THE UNRWA

DOCTOR DANIEL FARCAS
FELLOWSHIP RESEARCHER
FACULTY OF JEWISH STUDIES
MIDDLE EASTERN STUDIES
UNIVERSITY BAR ILAN

Antisemitism and the modern version anti zionism the classical explanation

Anti Semitism, the hatred and discrimination against Jews, has been a pervasive issue throughout history and continues to exist in various forms around the world today. The question of why there is antisemitism in all parts of the world is a complex one, with multiple factors contributing to this phenomenon.

One of the main drivers of antisemitism is the perpetuation of stereotypes and myths about Jews that have been passed down through generations. These stereotypes often portray Jews as greedy, manipulative, and untrustworthy, leading to a deep-seated mistrust and fear of the Jewish community. Additionally, the historical persecution of Jews, such as the Holocaust during World War II, has left a lasting impact on society and has fueled antisemitic sentiments.

Another factor that contributes to antisemitism is the perception of Jews as a threat to societal norms and values. Some individuals view Jews as outsiders who do not belong in their communities, leading to feelings of resentment and hostility towards them. This sense of otherness can be exacerbated by religious or cultural differences, further fueling antisemitic attitudes.

Furthermore, the rise of modern antisemitism, often disguised as anti-Zionism, has added a new dimension to the issue. Anti-Zionism is the opposition to the existence of the state of Israel and is often used as a guise for antisemitic rhetoric and actions. This form of antisemitism is particularly prevalent in political discourse and can lead to the demonization of Jews and their homeland.

It is important to note that there is no justification for the discrimination and hatred directed towards Jews in any case and in no one's special circumstances .

The idea that the existence of Jews is a problem is rooted in baseless prejudices and misconceptions. Jews, like any other group, deserve to be treated with respect and dignity, free from discrimination and persecution.

Antisemitism persists in all parts of the world due to a combination of historical, cultural, and political factors. The perpetuation of stereotypes, the fear of the other, and the rise of modern antisemitism all contribute to the prevalence of antisemitic attitudes. It is crucial for society to challenge these prejudices and work towards creating a more inclusive and tolerant world for all individuals, regardless of their background or beliefs.

The real cause of antisemitism, judeophobia and the modern version of hate the Anti Zionism, is that jews are the stone in the road that prevent others for happiness

The issue of antisemitism is a complex and deeply rooted phenomenon that has plagued societies for centuries. While there are various reasons commonly cited for the hatred towards Jews, such as the belief that they are responsible for the death of Jesus or that they are seen as selfish and greedy, these are not the true reasons behind antisemitism.

The underlying cause of antisemitism is hatred itself. Jews have often been scapegoated and targeted throughout history because they are seen as obstacles to progress, success, development and or happiness. This can be seen in historical events such as the Crusades, where Christians attempted to replace Jews, or the pogroms initiated by Alexander III in 1881 in Russia. In both cases, the goal was not to convert Jews but to exterminate them.

In more recent times, the conflict in the Middle East has also fueled antisemitism, with some Muslims viewing Jews as imperialists and oppressors. The state of Israel, in particular, has been a focal point of this hatred, as it is seen as a symbol of Western imperialism.

The Nazis' attempt to exterminate the Jewish population during the Holocaust was driven by a refusal to accept Jews as part of German society. Even someone as renowned as Albert Einstein faced discrimination and persecution because of his Jewish heritage.

Today, antisemitism continues to manifest itself in various forms, fueled by hatred and prejudice. The existence of Jews is often seen as a problem, regardless of their political beliefs, socioeconomic status, or religious practices.

Scholars and researchers have delved into the roots of antisemitism, seeking to understand and combat this pervasive form of discrimination. The work of academics like Professor Avi Gur, Einat Wilf, Professor Alan Derskovich, and others like Bernard Henry Levy enlightens the debate and allows many scholars and academics to contribute to this crucial discussion. All of them shed light on the complexities of antisemitism and its impact on society.

In fact antisemitism is a destructive force that must be confronted and challenged. By recognizing the true reasons behind this hatred and working towards greater understanding and tolerance, we can strive towards a more inclusive and harmonious society. It is essential to combat antisemitism in all its forms and stand against discrimination and prejudice in all its manifestations. The Jewish state of Israel is a vibrant democracy, a super developed and proud Jewish and Zionist country that deserves to be recognized and respected.

The two perspectives represent distinct views held by those who harbor antisemitic sentiments, with the modern form of antisemitism diverging significantly from traditional views. Traditional Antisemitism and the perspective of historical conception of antisemitism.

It has been based on negative stereotypes and myths about Jewish people, such as being selfish, greedy, overly capitalist, linked to Marxism or the left, too committed to work, or lazy. These stereotypes are found in fraudulent documents like the "Protocols of the Elders of Zion," which have perpetuated harmful myths and conspiracies about Jews for many years. Historically extreme and absurd accusations include claims that Jews poisoned the water and caused the Black Plague, or that for the Jewish celebration of Passover, Jews killed a young Catholic boy and used his blood to make traditional matzah.

Modern antisemitism is a complex and insidious form of discrimination that has evolved over time. Unlike traditional antisemitism, which focused on specific negative stereotypes and actions attributed to Jewish people, modern antisemitism takes a more abstract and systemic approach. It suggests that the mere existence of Jewish people is a hindrance to the success and well-being of others, regardless of their individual actions or characteristics.

One of the key features of modern antisemitism is the belief that Jews hold disproportionate power and influence in society. This belief is often rooted in conspiracy theories that portray Jews as controlling governments, financial institutions, and the media. These ideas have been perpetuated through the centuries and continue to fuel anti-Jewish sentiment in the modern world.

Another aspect of modern antisemitism is the idea that Jews are responsible for the world's problems. This can manifest in various ways, such as blaming Jews for economic downturns, political unrest, or social issues. By scapegoating Jews for these problems, individuals and groups are able to deflect responsibility and avoid addressing the root causes of these issues.

Furthermore, modern antisemitism often takes the form of anti-Zionism, which is the rejection of the Jewish state of Israel. While criticism of Israeli government policies is valid and important, anti-Zionism crosses the line into antisemitism when it denies the Jewish people the right to self-determination and demonizes Israel as a whole. This form of antisemitism is particularly prevalent in certain political and activist circles, where Israel is singled out for condemnation while other countries with similar or worse human rights records are ignored.

In conclusion, modern antisemitism is a multifaceted and pervasive form of discrimination that continues to impact Jewish communities around the world.

Modern Antisemitism, deep perspective

Anti Semitism, the hatred and discrimination against Jewish people, has taken on various forms throughout history. While traditional antisemitism focused on specific negative stereotypes and actions attributed to Jews, the modern perspective suggests that the mere existence of Jewish people is a hindrance to the happiness, success, or development of others. This shift in focus from individual actions to the idea that Jews are inherently problematic has profound implications for how Jewish people are perceived and treated in society.

The traditional form of antisemitism relied on specific stereotypes and actions, such as the belief that Jews were greedy, manipulative, or responsible for societal ills. This perspective suggested that if Jews were to change their behavior or beliefs to align more closely with societal norms, they might be accepted. However, the modern form of antisemitism takes a different approach, positing that there is no acceptable way for Jews to exist without being seen as an impediment to others' success. This viewpoint does not allow for any form of redemption or acceptance, even if Jews were to change their behavior or beliefs. It denies the possibility of being accepted as a proud Jew or a Zionist and rejects any notion that Jews could fit into society by conforming to certain standards or renouncing certain aspects of their identity.

The implications of this modern form of antisemitism are profound and troubling. By treating the Jewish identity itself as the problem, rather than any specific behavior or belief, this perspective dehumanizes Jewish people and denies them the possibility of positive relations or acceptance based on individual actions or characteristics. It casts Jewish people as eternal obstacles to societal progress, inherently incapable of being part of the solution. This dangerous viewpoint not only perpetuates harmful stereotypes and discrimination but also undermines the fundamental principles of equality and acceptance in society.

In conclusion, the shift from traditional antisemitism, which focused on specific negative traits and actions attributed to Jews, to the modern perspective, which suggests that the mere existence of Jewish people is a hindrance to others, has significant implications for how Jewish people are perceived and treated in society. By denying the possibility of acceptance based on individual actions or characteristics and treating the Jewish identity itself as the problem, this modern form of antisemitism is dehumanizing and dangerous. It is essential to challenge and confront this harmful perspective in order to promote understanding, acceptance, and equality for all individuals, regardless of their background or identity.

Addressing Anti Semitism

Antisemitism has been a pervasive issue throughout history, with Jewish people facing discrimination, persecution, and violence based on their religious and cultural identity. While traditional forms of antisemitism have been well-documented and understood, the modern form of antisemitism presents a new and insidious challenge. This modern perspective suggests that there is no acceptable way for Jews to exist without being seen as a hindrance to others' success. It denies the possibility of redemption or acceptance, even if Jews were to change their behavior or beliefs. This perspective eliminates any possibility of positive relations or acceptance based on individual actions or characteristics, treating the Jewish identity itself as the problem.

The modern form of antisemitism is deeply dehumanizing and dangerous because it casts Jewish people as eternal obstacles to societal progress. By denying the possibility of acceptance or understanding, this perspective perpetuates harmful stereotypes and prejudices. It suggests that Jews are inherently incapable of being part of the solution, regardless of their actions or beliefs. This not only marginalizes Jewish individuals but also undermines the principles of equality and tolerance in society.

Antisemitism requires a deep understanding of both historical and contemporary contexts. It is essential to recognize the persistence of traditional antisemitic stereotypes and the ways in which they have adapted to new societal norms and conditions. However, the modern form of antisemitism represents a shift in focus that is equally harmful, if not more so, because it offers no path for acceptance or understanding. It is crucial to challenge and confront this perspective, advocating for inclusivity, diversity, and respect for all individuals, regardless of their religious or cultural background.

Indeed the modern form of antisemitism poses a significant threat to Jewish individuals and communities, perpetuating harmful stereotypes and prejudices. By denying the possibility of acceptance or understanding, this perspective undermines the principles of equality and tolerance in society. It is essential to address and confront this form of antisemitism, advocating for inclusivity, diversity, and respect for all individuals. Only through education, awareness, and activism can we work towards a more inclusive and accepting society for all.

Combating both forms of antisemitism involves robust education, critical thinking, and proactive efforts to promote inclusivity and understanding. It is essential to challenge and debunk these harmful myths and stereotypes, whether they are rooted in historical prejudices or modern reinterpretations. Understanding the nuances and evolution of antisemitic thought is crucial for developing effective strategies to counteract it and foster a more inclusive and accepting society.

It's not possible to understand the human rights organizations, unfair and biased organizations, the animosity against Israel in the United Nations and certainly the incredible case of antisemitism that has been the existence and management of UNRWA.

The two perspectives represent distinct views held by those who harbor antisemitic sentiments, with the modern form of antisemitism diverging significantly from traditional views.

Traditional Antisemitism. The first perspective is the historical conception of antisemitism.

It has been based on negative stereotypes and myths about Jewish people, such as being selfish, greedy, overly capitalist, linked to Marxism or the left, too committed to work, or lazy. These stereotypes are found in fraudulent documents like the "Protocols of the Elders of Zion," which have perpetuated harmful myths and conspiracies about Jews for many years. Historically extreme and absurd accusations include claims that Jews poisoned the water and caused the Black

Plague, or that for the Jewish celebration of Passover, Jews killed a young Catholic boy and used his blood to make traditional

Anti Semitism and old new illnesses

Addressing any kind of forms of antisemitism requires a deep understanding of both historical and contemporary contexts. Traditional antisemitic stereotypes have persisted for centuries, often adapting to new societal norms and conditions. However, the modern form described here represents a shift in focus that is just as harmful, if not more so, because it offers no path for acceptance or understanding.Combating both forms of antisemitism involves robust education, critical thinking, and proactive efforts to promote inclusivity and understanding. It is essential to challenge and debunk these harmful myths and stereotypes, whether they are rooted in historical prejudices or modern reinterpretations. Understanding the nuances and evolution of antisemitic thought is crucial for developing effective strategies to counteract it and foster a more inclusive and accepting society.

Promoting Arabs terrorism in Palestine

The Mufti al Hajmani, a prominent Palestinian leader during the early 20th century, is correctly associated with promoting terrorism against Jews and advocating for the boycott of Jewish businesses. His alliance with the German Nazis during World War II further solidified his reputation as a controversial figure in history, posing a threat to the Arab population in Palestine. He used his influence to incite violence against Jewish communities, leading to numerous attacks and acts of terrorism. His calls for the boycott of Jewish businesses were aimed at economically. It could be affirmed that the Mufti was indeed the pioneer of the antisemitic famous BDS. The truth is that he deserves the credit for that and not always have been a real recognition to his strong commitment to jews haters

The Mufti's anti-Semitic views were deeply ingrained in his belief in isolating the Jewish population and weakening their presence in the region.

During World War II, the Mufti formed a strategic alliance with the German Nazis, viewing them as potential allies in the fight against British colonial rule in Palestine. He met with high-ranking Nazi officials, including Adolf Hitler, and actively supported their anti-Semitic policies. This alliance further fueled his anti-Jewish rhetoric and actions, leading to increased violence and persecution against Jewish communities.

The Mufti's collaboration with the Nazis has been widely condemned by historians and scholars, as it not only perpetuated anti-Semitism but also contributed to the atrocities committed during the Holocaust. His actions have had a lasting impact on the relationship between Muslims and Jews, reinforcing negative stereotypes and deepening historical tensions.

The Mufti's terrorism against Jews, boycott of Jewish businesses, and the alliance with the German Nazis have left a dark mark on history. His actions have fueled hatred and violence, perpetuating divisions between different religious and ethnic groups. It is important to remember that Arabs in Palestine were more engaged in preventing the establishment of a Jewish state than in the construction of their own state.

The Mufti's promotion of violence and discrimination against Jews serves as a reminder of the dangers of extremism and intolerance. His actions highlight the importance of promoting peace, understanding, and cooperation among different communities. By learning from the mistakes of the past, we can strive to build a more inclusive and harmonious society for future generations.

2.Lost Palestinian Opportunities

A. The Peel Commission

The Peel Commission, established in 1936, was a British Royal Commission tasked with investigating the causes of the Arab revolt in Palestine and making recommendations for future governance of the region. The Commission's Commission Report, published in 1937, proposed the partition of Palestine into separate Jewish and Arab states, with an international zone in Jerusalem. While the Peel Commission's recommendations were not implemented, they represented a missed opportunity for a peaceful resolution to the conflict between Jews and Arabs in Palestine.

The Peel Commission's proposal for partition was met with strong opposition from the Arab leaders. The Arab Higher Committee rejected the Just outright, arguing that it did not adequately address the rights of the Arab population in Palestine. Jewish leaders, while initially open to the idea of partition, ultimately rejected the plan as well, as they believed it did not provide for a viable Jewish state with sufficient territory.

Despite the failure of the Peel Commission's recommendations, the proposal for partition represented a potential opportunity for a peaceful resolution to the conflict in Palestine. By creating separate Jewish and Arab states, the Commission sought to address the competing national aspirations of both communities. However, the rejection of the plan by both sides ultimately led to continued violence and unrest in the region.

The Peel Commission was not the only missed opportunity for peace in Palestine. Throughout the 20th century, various proposals for partition, federation, and other forms of governance were put forward, only to be rejected by one or both sides. The United Nations Partition Plan of 1947, which proposed the creation of separate Jewish and Arab states in Palestine, was another such opportunity that was ultimately rejected by Arab leaders.

The failure to seize these opportunities for peace in Palestine has had lasting consequences for the region. The ongoing conflict between Israelis and Palestinians, marked by violence, displacement, and human rights abuses, is a direct result of the failure to find a just and lasting solution to the competing national aspirations of both communities.

In conclusion, the Peel Commission and other lost opportunities for peace in Palestine represent a tragic chapter in the history of the region. The failure to find a just and equitable solution to the conflict between Jews and Arabs has led to decades of violence and suffering for both communities. It is imperative that all parties involved in the conflict work towards a peaceful resolution that respects the rights and aspirations of both Israelis and Palestinians.

A. The partition of the United Nations

The partition of the United Nations (UN) in 1947 was a significant event in the history of the Israeli-Palestinian conflict. The partition plan, also known as UN Resolution 181, called for the division of British Mandate Palestine into separate Jewish and Arab states, with Jerusalem as an international city. While the plan was accepted by the Jewish leadership, it was rejected by the Arab states and the Palestinian leadership, leading to the outbreak of the first Arab-Israeli war in 1948.

The partition of the UN was a missed opportunity for the Palestinians for several reasons.

Furthermore, the partition of the UN did not take into account all and each one of the complex religious and cultural ties that both Jews had to the land of Palestine. Jerusalem, in particular, is a city of great significance to Jews, and the partition plan's proposal to make it an international city did not adequately address the competing claims to the city.

Overall, the partition of the UN was a missed opportunity for the Palestinians to achieve a just and lasting solution to the conflict, but they chose not to find a way of understanding with the Jews. Not before, not after, not in the middle, indeed the answer was always the same. As doctor Wilf affirmed we should give the Palestinians the credits for always telling the truth; they are not today and certainly not yesterday willing to accept a Jewish state no matter in which borders.

The partition of the UN in 1947 was a missed opportunity for the Palestinians to achieve a fair and equitable resolution to the Israeli-Palestinian conflict. The plan's failure to address key issues such as land distribution, refugee rights, and religious and cultural ties to the land has had lasting consequences for the region. It is important for the international community to learn from the mistakes of the past and work towards a just and lasting solution to the conflict that takes into account the rights and aspirations of both Israelis and Palestinians.

• C. Oslo Accords

The Oslo Accords, signed in 1993, were seen as a historic opportunity for peace agreement between the Israelis and Palestinians. The agreement, brokered by US President Bill Clinton and Israeli Prime Minister Yitzhak Rabin, aimed to establish a framework for resolving the long-standing conflict in the region. However, despite the initial optimism surrounding the Accords, the peace process ultimately faltered, leaving Palestinians feeling as though they had lost a crucial opportunity for a just and lasting resolution to the conflict.

One of the key reasons for the failure of the Oslo Accords was the lack of trust between the two parties. While the agreement called for mutual recognition and cooperation, Israelis remained deeply suspicious and with good reasons. This lack of trust was exacerbated by a series of violent incidents, Palestinian terrorism support, including suicide bombings and israelis assassination, which further eroded the fragile peace process.

Furthermore, the assassination of Prime Minister Rabin in 1995 dealt a severe blow to the peace process. Rabin, who was a strong advocate for peace and a key architect of the Oslo Accords, was seen as a moderate voice within the Israeli government. His death not only created a power vacuum within the Israeli leadership but also emboldened hardline elements within the Israeli society who opposed any concessions to the Palestinians.

In the years following the collapse of Israeli citizens' hope was directly proportional to the growth of Palestine terrorist acts.

In conclusion, the Oslo Accords represented a historic opportunity for peace between Israelis and Palestinians. However, the peace process ultimately faltered, because Palestinians had lost a crucial opportunity for a just and lasting resolution to the conflict, essentially Palestinian never wanted a two state solution.

Yasser Arafat was first at all a murdered and recognized terrorist .The former leader of the Palestinian Liberation Organization (PLO), is often remembered as a blood cowardly murder, and a controversial figure in the history of the Israeli-Palestinian conflict. Arafat, who was born in Cairo in 1929, rose to prominence as a key figure in the Palestinian nationalist movement and became known for his role in organizing and leading acts of terrorism against Jews and Israel.

Throughout his career, Arafat was responsible for numerous terrorist attacks, including the infamous Munich Olympics massacre in 1972, where 11 Israeli athletes were killed by Palestinian terrorists. Arafat's tactics of violence and terror were seen as a means to achieve his ultimate goal of establishing a Palestinian state and gaining independence from the so-called "Israeli occupation."

Despite his violent methods and his full commitment to terrorism, Arafat was also involved in peace negotiations with Israel, particularly during the Oslo Accords in the 1990s. These negotiations led with the "nahib" attitude of the Israeli delegation to the establishment of the Palestinian Authority and the recognition of the PLO as the legitimate representative of the Palestinian people. Such kind of wishful thinking could be understandable but it was indeed a dangerous move with an awful outcome.The west listened only the English speeches and because Arafat was ,absurdly awarded with the Nobel Peace Prize in 1994 "for his efforts in promoting peace in the region". Absolutely false and really against all real evidence.

"I'm writing it now and I can see how wrong I was,because I also wanted to believe that yes, the Palestinian were indeed committed to peace and as important as this, they wanted a Palestinian state side by side with the Jewish state and not instead of Israel".

"I'm guilty as many liberals and left wing militants who wanted so much to believe in a peace process that were deft to the real message of the Palestinians. And their request was the same that you can hear in any European or American country "from the river to the sea". And free from what? Free from a Jewish sovereignty."

Arafat's commitment to peace was never truly sincere, he always was a professional player in the art of occuring the truth, in order that the west could believe that he was willing to be a real partner in the peace process. Indeed, he always continued to support and fund terrorist activities against Jews worldwide and Israel in particular. His refusal to fully renounce violence and his ambiguous stance on the recognition of Israel as a state, hindered the progress of the peace process.

D. Arafat saying no to a Palestinian state with Jerusalem like it´s capital

In 2000, Arafat was presented with a historic opportunity to establish a Palestinian state alongside Israel during negotiations with then-Israeli Prime Minister Ehud Barak and US President Bill Clinton. The offer included the establishment of a Palestinian state with East Jerusalem as its capital and a significant portion of the West Bank and Gaza Strip under Palestinian control. However, Arafat rejected the offer, claiming it did not meet the aspirations of the Palestinian people.

Arafat's decision to walk away from the negotiating table was seen as a missed opportunity to achieve a lasting peace in the region. His refusal to compromise and his continued support for terrorism only served to further escalate tensions between Israelis and Palestinians, leading to a renewed cycle of violence and

Yasser Arafat's legacy as a terrorist leader and a symbol of Palestinian "resistance" is a complex and controversial one. While he played a significant role in the struggle for Palestinian independence, his tactics of violence and terrorism and definitely his reluctance to fully commit to peace ultimately hindered the progress towards a lasting resolution of the Israeli-Palestinian conflict. Arafat's refusal to seize the opportunity for peace with Israel, not one but many times especially during the negotiations with Barak and Clinton in 2000 serves as a stark reminder of the consequences of prioritizing violence over diplomacy.

E. Abbas Missing Opportunity with Olmert

In the realm of international diplomacy, opportunities for peace are often fleeting and must be seized upon when they arise. One such opportunity presented itself in 2008 when Palestinian President Mahmoud Abbas met with Israeli Prime Minister Ehud Olmert to discuss a potential peace agreement. However, Abbas ultimately failed to capitalize on this chance for progress, and the two leaders were unable to reach a lasting resolution to the Israeli-Palestinian conflict.

The meeting between Abbas and Olmert took place against a backdrop of ongoing violence and unrest in the region. Both leaders were under pressure from their respective constituencies to find a way to end the conflict and establish a lasting peace. Olmert, in particular, had expressed a willingness to make significant concessions in order to reach a peace agreement, including the division of Jerusalem and the establishment of a Palestinian state.

Abbas, on the other hand, was hesitant to make concessions, fearing that he would be seen as betraying the Palestinian cause. Despite this, he had an opportunity to negotiate with Olmert and potentially secure a favorable agreement for the Palestinian people. However, Abbas failed to take advantage of this opportunity, and the talks ultimately broke down without a resolution being reached.

There are several reasons why Abbas may have missed this opportunity with Olmert. One possible explanation is that he was under pressure from hardline factions within the Palestinian Authority who were opposed to making any concessions to Israel. Abbas may have feared that agreeing to a peace deal with Olmert would have led to a backlash from these groups and threatened his own political survival.

Additionally, Abbas may have been worry to have the same fate that Anwar Sadat had because he signed a peace treaty with Israel, to be cruelly assassinated by his own people.

Overall, Abbas's failure to capitalize on the opportunity presented by his meeting with Olmert was a missed chance for progress in the Israeli-Palestinian conflict. The Palestinian leaders were unable to reach a lasting peace agreement, and the conflict continues to this day. It serves as a reminder of the importance of seizing upon opportunities for peace when they arise, and the consequences of failing to do so. Abbas's missed opportunity with Olmert is a cautionary tale for future leaders involved in international diplomacy, highlighting the need to act decisively and courageously in pursuit of peace.

Not only Palestinian losing opportunities, the case of Arab Spring.

The Arab Spring, which began in late 2010, was a transformative period in the history of the Middle East and North Africa. It was a time when people across the region came together to demand political reform, economic opportunity, and social justice. The protests, uprisings, and revolutions that swept through countries like Tunisia, Egypt, Libya, and Syria were fueled by a deep-seated desire for change and a rejection of the authoritarian regimes that had long oppressed their citizens.

One of the key factors that contributed to the outbreak of the Arab Spring was the widespread dissatisfaction with the political and economic conditions in many Arab countries. High levels of unemployment, corruption, and lack of political freedom had created a sense of frustration and disillusionment among the population. The spark that ignited the protests was the self-immolation of Mohamed Bouazizi, a Tunisian street vendor who set himself on fire in protest against government corruption and harassment. His act of defiance galvanized the Tunisian people and set off a chain reaction of protests that quickly spread to other countries in the region.

The Arab Spring was characterized by a sense of hope and optimism, as people from all walks of life came together to demand change. The protesters were united in their calls for greater political freedom, economic opportunity, and social justice. They were inspired by the belief that they could create a better future for themselves and their children, free from the oppression and corruption that had plagued their countries for so long.

The Arab Spring also highlighted the power of social media and technology in mobilizing and organizing protests. Platforms like Facebook, Twitter, and YouTube played a crucial role in spreading information, coordinating actions, and raising awareness about the injustices faced by the people in the region. The use of social media allowed protesters to bypass government censorship and connect with like-minded individuals both within their own countries and around the world.

However, the Arab Spring also faced significant challenges and setbacks. The initial wave of protests in Tunisia and Egypt led to the ousting of long-time dictators Zine El Abidine Ben Ali and Hosni Mubarak, but the transitions to democracy that followed were fraught with difficulties. In Libya and Syria, the uprisings descended into brutal civil wars that have caused immense suffering and destruction. The hopes and dreams of the Arab Spring were dashed as the region descended into chaos and violence.

Despite these challenges, the legacy of the Arab Spring is mixed. The protests and uprisings of 2010-2011 sparked a wave of change that continues to reverberate throughout the region. The people of the Middle East and North Africa have shown that they are not afraid to stand up for their rights and demand a better future for themselves and their children. The Arab Spring has faltered in many countries bringing pain, disaster and destruction.

The Arab Spring, like the European Spring of Nations, was a series of protests and uprisings that swept across the Arab world in 2010 and 2011, with the aim of bringing about political and social change. However, unlike the European Spring of Nations, the Arab Spring has faced setbacks and challenges that have hindered its success.

In countries such as Egypt and Syria, the initial optimism and hope of the protests gave way to violence, repression, and civil war. In Egypt, the ousting of President Hosni Mubarak in 2011 was followed by a period of political instability, with the military eventually taking control of the government. In Syria, what began as peaceful protests against President Bashar al-Assad's regime quickly escalated into a brutal civil war that has claimed hundreds of thousands of lives and displaced millions of people.

In other countries, such as Tunisia and Libya, the transition to democracy has been slow and difficult. In Tunisia, the birthplace of the Arab Spring, the country has made no significant progress towards democracy, with still a long road ahead to free and fair elections and a permanent decision regarding a new constitution. However, political instability and economic challenges continue to plague the country. In Libya, the overthrow of Muammar Gaddafi in 2011 led to a power vacuum that has been filled by rival militias and factions, leading to ongoing violence and instability.

One of the key issues that has hindered the success of the Arab Spring is the deep-rooted conflicts in the region, particularly the Israel-Palestine conflict. This conflict, which has been ongoing for decades, is not simply a territorial dispute, as some may believe. It is a complex and multifaceted conflict rooted in deep-seated historical, religious, and political differences between Jews and Arabs.

The Israel-Palestine conflict is a deeply rooted issue that has been ongoing for decades. In their analysis of this conflict, Einat Wilf and Aviv Gur argue that the fundamental disagreement between Jews and Arabs is the aspiration of Jews to have a Jewish state, while Arabs oppose the existence of a Jewish state. This fundamental difference in goals has made finding a resolution incredibly difficult and has contributed to the ongoing instability in the region.

The conflict between Israel and Palestine dates back to the late 19th century, when Jewish immigrants began to settle in the region that was then part of the Ottoman Empire. The Zionist movement, which sought to establish a Jewish homeland in Palestine, clashed with the Arab population who saw the land as their own. This clash of national aspirations laid the foundation for the conflict that continues to this day.

The creation of the state of Israel in 1948 further exacerbated tensions between Jews and Arabs. The Arab states rejected the United Nations partition plan that would have created separate Jewish and Arab states in Palestine, leading to a war that resulted in the displacement of hundreds of thousands of Palestinians. This event, known as the Nakba, continues to be a source of resentment and anger among Palestinians.

Since then, the conflict has been marked by periods of violence and attempts at peace negotiations. The Oslo Accords in the 1990s aimed to establish a framework for a two-state solution, but ultimately failed to bring about lasting peace. The continued expansion of Israeli settlements in the West Bank and the blockade of Gaza have further complicated efforts to find a resolution to the conflict.

Wilf and Gur argue that the fundamental disagreement between Jews and Arabs over the existence of a Jewish state lies at the heart of the conflict. For Jews, the establishment of Israel represents a long-held dream of self-determination and security in the wake of centuries of persecution. For Arabs, the creation of Israel is seen as a colonial project that has displaced and marginalized the indigenous population.

This fundamental difference in goals has made finding a resolution to the conflict incredibly difficult. Both sides have deep historical and emotional attachments to the land, making compromise a challenging prospect. The ongoing violence and mistrust between Israelis and Palestinians only serve to further entrench these differences and make the prospect of peace seem increasingly remote.

In conclusion, the Israel-Palestine conflict is not a complex issue, but rather a deeply rooted one that stems from the fundamental disagreement between Jews and Arabs over the existence of a Jewish state. Until Palestinianscan find a way to reconcile with the existence of the state of Israel, the conflict is likely to continue unabated. Only through dialogue, understanding, and a willingness to compromise can a lasting peace be achieved in the region.

The establishment of the State of Israel in 1948 was a pivotal moment in the conflict, as it fulfilled the long-held dream of the Jewish people to have a homeland of their own.Regardless of what are the motivation of one side or the other are just or injust, this is the essence of the conflict. However, this was met with opposition from the Arab population in the region, who s. VPN aw the creation of Israel as an unjust usurpation of their land. This fundamental disagreement over the legitimacy of a Jewish state has been a major obstacle to finding a peaceful resolution to the conflict.

The Israeli-Palestinian conflict is not a territorial dispute, but a deeply entrenched ideological and existential conflict. For Jews, Israel represents a safe haven and a symbol of national identity, while for many Arabs, the existence of Israel is seen as a constant reminder of historical injustices and ongoing oppression. This clash of narratives has created a deep-seated animosity between the two sides, making it difficult to find common ground for peace.

The ongoing instability in the region can be attributed in part to this fundamental disagreement over the existence of a Jewish state. The refusal of many Arab states to recognize Israel's right to exist has led to decades of conflict, violence, and mistrust. The lack of mutual recognition and acceptance of each other's right to self-determination has perpetuated a cycle of violence and retaliation that has only served to deepen the divide between the two sides.

In order to move towards a resolution of the Israel-Palestine conflict, it is essential for both Jews and Arabs to acknowledge and respect each other's legitimate aspirations and rights. This will require a willingness to engage in dialogue, compromise, and reconciliation. It is only through mutual recognition and understanding that a lasting peace can be achieved in the region. But this is absolutely impossible when the Palestinians want more to prevent the existence of the state of Israel rather than to build their own state.

The fundamental disagreement between Jews and Arabs over the existence of a Jewish state has been a major obstacle to finding a resolution to the Israel-Palestine conflict. This deep-rooted ideological conflict has contributed to the ongoing instability in the region and has made it difficult to find a path towards peace. It is essential for both sides to acknowledge each other's legitimate aspirations and rights in order to move towards a peaceful resolution of the conflict.

While the Arab Spring initially brought hope and optimism for change in the Arab world, it has faced significant challenges and setbacks. The deep-rooted conflicts in the region, particularly the Israel-Palestine conflict, have hindered the success of the protests and have contributed to ongoing violence, repression, and political instability. Moving forward, it will be important for the international community to continue to support efforts towards peace and stability in the region.

The Israel-Palestine conflict is not a simple territorial dispute, but a deeply rooted issue that has been ongoing for decades. In their analysis of this conflict, EInat Wilf and Haviv Gur argue that the fundamental disagreement between Jews and Arabs is the aspiration of Jews to have a Jewish state, while Arabs oppose the existence of a Jewish state.

Difference in goals has made finding a resolution incredibly difficult and has contributed to the ongoing instability in the region.

The establishment of the State of Israel in 1948 was a pivotal moment in the conflict, as it fulfilled the long-held dream of the Jewish people to have a homeland of their own. However, this was met with opposition from the Arab population in the region, who saw the creation of Israel as an unjust usurpation of their land. This fundamental disagreement over the legitimacy of a Jewish state has been a major obstacle to finding a peaceful resolution to the conflict.

The Israeli-Palestinian conflict is not a territorial dispute, but a deeply entrenched ideological and existential conflict. For Jews, Israel represents a safe haven and a symbol of national identity, while for many Arabs, the existence of Israel is seen as a constant reminder of historical injustices and ongoing oppression. This clash of narratives has created a deep-seated animosity between the two sides, making it difficult to find common ground for peace.

The ongoing instability in the region can be attributed in part to this fundamental disagreement over the existence of a Jewish state. The refusal of many Arab states to recognize Israel's right to exist has led to decades of conflict, violence, and mistrust. The lack of mutual recognition and acceptance of Each other's right to self-determination has perpetuated a cycle of violence and retaliation that has only served to deepen the divide between the two sides.

In order to move towards a resolution of the Israel-Palestine conflict, it is essential to acknowledge and respect each other's legitimate aspirations and rights. This will require a willingness to engage in dialogue, compromise, and reconciliation. It is only through mutual recognition and understanding that a lasting peace can be achieved in the region. Jews were, and are people willing to have a deep historical and cultural connection to the land.

The fundamental disagreement between Jews and Arabs is over the existence of a Jewish state has been a major obstacle to finding a resolution to the Israel-Palestine conflict. This deep-rooted ideological conflict has contributed to the ongoing instability in the region and has made it difficult to find a path towards peace. It is essential for both sides to acknowledge each other's legitimate aspirations and rights in order to move towards a peaceful resolution of the conflict.

Despite the challenges and setbacks faced by the Arab Spring and the Israel-Palestine conflict, there is still reason for optimism in the Middle East. The region is home to a young and dynamic population that is increasingly demanding greater political freedom, economic opportunity, and social justice. The Arab Spring may not have led to immediate and lasting change, but it has sparked a new wave of activism and engagement that will continue to shape the future.

The Arab Spring and the Israel-Palestine conflict are just two examples of the complex and interconnected challenges facing the Middle East. While there are no easy solutions to these issues, there is reason for optimism in the region. By addressing the root causes of conflict, promoting dialogue and reconciliation, and supporting the aspirations of the people, the Middle East can overcome its challenges and build a more peaceful and prosperous future.

The Arab Spring brought some hope for some people hoping for a real change and a new social contract between rulers and the ruled in the Middle East. However, the challenges and setbacks faced by the movement have highlighted the deep-rooted issues and complexities in the region. The conflict between Israel and Palestine is just one example of the broader challenges facing the Middle East as it undergoes a period of transformation.

As the region continues to grapple with these challenges, it is important to recognize the complexities and nuances of the conflicts and issues at play. Only by understanding the root causes of these conflicts can we hope to find

more stable and peaceful land.

An deeply rooted issue that has its origins in the early 20th century. The establishment of the state of Israel in 1948 led to the displacement of hundreds of thousands of Palestinians, who became refugees in neighboring countries. The subsequent wars and conflicts between Israel and its Arab neighbors, as well as the ongoing occupation of Palestinian territories, have only served to deepen the animosity and distrust between the two sides.

The Israeli-Palestinian conflict is not a territorial dispute, but also a clash of national identities, historical narratives, and religious beliefs. Jews have legitimate claims to the land, and have suffered greatly as a result of the conflict, but indeed their history is a long and complex attempt to exterminate the jews from the face of the earth.

The international community has tried to mediate and find a solution to the conflict, but so far, a lasting peace agreement has remained elusive.

As Einat Wilf affirmed, the West had chosen to feel well instead of acting good. They have chosen to finance UNRWA instead to face the terrorist roots of the questioned Palestinian organization.

The Middle East is a region of great diversity, with a rich history and culture. It is also a region of great complexity, with deep-seated conflicts and challenges. The issues facing the Middle East today are not just political or economic, but also social, cultural, and religious. The conflicts in the region, including the Israeli-Palestinian conflict, are a reflection of these broader challenges and transformations.

In order to understand the Middle East and its future course, it is important to consider the historical context, the shared experiences, and the complex challenges facing the region. The parallels with Europe in the 19th century provide some insights into the magnitude of the transformation that the Arab world is undergoing. The conflicts in the Middle East, particularly the Israeli-Palestinian conflict, are a reflection of these broader changes and challenges.

The Middle East is a region with deep-seated conflicts and challenges. The issues facing the region today are not just political or economic, but also social, cultural, and religious. The conflicts in the Middle East, including the Israeli-Palestinian conflict, are a reflection of these broader challenges and transformations. It is important to consider the historical context and the shared experiences in order to understand the Middle East and its future course.

A political reform, and for greater representation in the course of the Arab Spring were tied with the rise of sectarian sentiments and the demand to find proper political expression for those separate groups.

Once the century-old structures were exposed in their artificiality, the old identities that laid low for nearly a century rose to the surface to claim their due. In Europe, these were called "nations" and "peoples;" in the Middle East they are called "tribes," "sects," and "ethnicities" but the principle remains the same. Groups that claim cohesiveness based on history, language, culture, and kinship are rising up, demanding that political structures that do not give expression to these groupings – whether they are multiethnic empires, states artificially created by colonial forces, or small principalities – give way to new structures that better reflect the groups' demands for more cohesive political expression.

Just as the empires did not easily give way to the demands of the subject peoples for national expression, and just as Germany and Italy did not emerge from disparate principalities without bloody battles, it would be wrong to expect the post-World War I order in the Middle East to simply fade away in the face of The identities created during the century between the breakup of the Ottoman Empire and the Arab Spring, despite being relatively new, cannot be written off easily. Current actors in the Middle East have grown up as Syrians, Iraqis, Jordanians, and Saudis, and that has power. These new identities also have the power of interests: powerful economic and military interests are tied to keeping the new identities alive, and they will not give in without a very bloody fight.

A New Power Architecture

It's supposed to be a strong connection between their national identities and their foreign policy ambitions

The trees are Turkey, Iran, and Saudi Arabia. Each of these countries has a distinct national identity rooted in history, culture, and religion, and each seeks to expand its influence in the region based on these identities.

Turkey, for example, is supposed to see itself as a bridge between Europe and Asia, with a history that spans both continents. But Mr

Erdoğan seems to be busy promoting antisemitic theories and anti Israel propaganda .It's Ottoman past gives it a sense of historical greatness and a desire to reclaim its role as a regional power. Turkey's foreign policy is driven by a desire to protect its interests in the region, including its support for Sunni Muslim groups in Syria and its opposition to Kurdish separatism.

Iran, on the other hand, sees itself as the guardian of Shia Islam and the leader of the Islamic world. Its foreign policy is driven by a desire to protect Shia communities in the region and to counter the influence of Sunni powers like Saudi Arabia. Iran's support for Shia militias in Iraq and Syria, as well as its nuclear program, are all part of its strategy to expand its influence in the region.

Saudi Arabia, meanwhile, sees itself as the leader of the Sunni Muslim world and the guardian of the holy sites of Islam. Its foreign policy is driven by a desire to counter the influence of Shia powers like Iran and to protect its interests in the region. Saudi Arabia's support for Sunni groups in Syria and its intervention in Yemen are all part of its strategy to expand its influence in the region.

These three countries are engaged in a complex web of alliances and rivalries, with each seeking to outmaneuver the others to expand its influence. Turkey, for example, has formed alliances with Qatar and Russia to counter the influence of Saudi Arabia and Iran. Iran, meanwhile, has formed alliances with Syria and Hezbollah to counter the influence of Turkey and Saudi Arabia. And Saudi Arabia has formed alliances with the United Arab Emirates and Egypt to counter the influence of Iran and Turkey.

This new architecture of the Middle East is marked by shifting alliances, covert and overt struggles, and a strong connection between national identities and foreign policy ambitions. Like in 19th century Europe, the top mid-sized regional powers are engaged in a complex game of power politics, with each seeking to expand its influence and protect its interests in the region. As the Cold War's domination of the geopolitics of the Middle East recedes, this new architecture is likely to continue to evolve, with Turkey, Iran, and Saudi Arabia at its center.

history of being subject to the Ottoman Empire – Turkey, Iran, and Israel – are those that enjoy the most distinct sense of national identity. Turkey, for obvious y went through the difficult process of establishing itself as a country with a dist

Palestinian people.

As the heir to the seat of the Ottoman Empire it is a natural regional power in the areas that were previously under imperial control. While there is still much to be done in terms of greater openness, democratization, and national expression for minorities, Turkey's regime and coherence are only marginally threatened by the delayed "Ottoman Spring." Turkey is therefore well placed to play the role of a regional power.

MINORITY REPORT: JEWS ARE THE FIRST VICTIMS, BUT NEVER THE LAST

Doctor Wilf work is a good example of how to deal with the Middle east , she shared her experience

She wrote "just the other day, my Christian Lebanese colleague expressed a sentiment that struck me deeply. He said, "We, the Arabs of the Middle East, miss you – the Jews." This statement, coming from a member of a community that has historically been at odds with the Jewish people, was both surprising and thought-provoking."

She continued to share "as he elaborated on his statement, my colleague explained that the expulsion and forced exodus of nearly a million Jews from the Arab Middle East over sixty years ago was just the beginning of a larger trend of persecution and displacement in the region. He pointed to the current wave of Islamic brutality, genocide, and ethnic cleansing that is targeting Christian communities in areas where the Islamic State is gaining power. Just as the Jewish communities were uprooted from their homes, these Christian communities – some of which have existed since before the rise of Islam – are now facing a similar fate."

The Middle East has long been a region of great religious and cultural diversity, with both Jewish and Christian communities having deep roots in the area. However, the experiences of these two groups in the region have been marked by striking parallels, particularly in terms of the persecution and violence they have faced at the hands of extremist forces.

Both the Jewish and Christian communities in the Middle East have been targeted for their religious beliefs and cultural identities. Throughout history, both groups have been subjected to discrimination, violence, and persecution based on their faith. This persecution has often been fueled by extremist ideologies that seek to eradicate or marginalize religious minorities in the region.

One of the most tragic parallels between the experiences of the Jewish and Christian communities in the Middle East is the violence and displacement they have endured. Both groups have been forced to flee their homes and seek refuge in other countries due to threats of violence and persecution. The rise of extremist groups in the region has only exacerbated this situation, leading to increased levels of violence and instability for both communities.

It is particularly poignant that my colleague, a member of the Arab Christian community, can see and acknowledge these similarities. Despite the historical tensions between different religious groups in the region, it is heartening to see individuals who are able to recognize and empathize with the struggles of others. This speaks to the depth of the tragedy unfolding in the Middle East, where religious and cultural differences have been weaponized to justify violence and oppression.

In order to address the challenges facing both the Jewish and Christian communities in the Middle East, it is essential for the international community to stand in solidarity with these groups and work towards promoting religious tolerance and coexistence in the region. By acknowledging the parallels between their experiences and advocating for their rights, we can help to create a more inclusive and peaceful future for all religious minorities in the Middle East.

In conclusion, the parallels between the experiences of the Jewish and Christian communities in the Middle East are indeed striking. Both groups have faced persecution and violence at the hands of extremist forces, and both have been forced to endure displacement and instability as a result. It is crucial for us to recognize and address these challenges in order to promote religious tolerance and coexistence in the region. Only by standing together in solidarity can we hope to create a more peaceful and inclusive future for all religious minorities in the Middle East.

She expressed its sadness, and remarked "The plight of the Christian communities in the Middle East is a stark reminder of the fragility of religious and cultural diversity in the face of extremism. It is a reminder that the forces of intolerance and hatred can quickly erase centuries of coexistence and mutual respect. It is a reminder that we must remain vigilant in the face of such threats, and that we must work together to protect and preserve the rich tapestry of identities that make up our world."

In reflecting on my colleague's words, I am reminded of the importance of solidarity and empathy in the face of adversity. As we witness the suffering of our fellow human beings, regardless of their religious or cultural background, we must stand together in support and solidarity. We must reject the forces of division and hatred, and work towards a future where all people can live in peace and harmony.

In conclusion, doctor Wilf's mcolleague's statement serves as a powerful reminder of the shared experiences and struggles of different religious and cultural communities in the Middle East. It is a call to action for all of us to stand together in the face of intolerance and violence, and to work towards a future where diversity and coexistence are celebrated and protected. Only by coming together in solidarity can we hope to build a more just and peaceful world for all.

Doctor Einat Wilf added "He said that he is terrified to think of an Arab Middle East without minorities. He expressed fear that the intolerance demonstrated towards the Jews decades ago is now being turned towards almost all other minorities from Christians to Alawites to Shiites to the Sunni Muslims who fail to uphold the demented standards for Muslim piety set by the Islamic State.

My Arab colleague was brave enough to admit this simple truth that the world has learned over and over again, and yet seems to never internalize: It starts with the Jews. It never ends with the Jews.

Rising tides of hatred, intolerance, and brutality are not satisfied once they have rid society of its Jews. Sooner or later, others will follow.

Not only does it never end with the Jews. It is never really about the Jews. That is why it never ends with them. Hatred of Jews is about those who hate – not about those who are hated.

When the "Jewish Question" was discussed in Europe of the 19th century, it was not really the Jewish Question – rather it was the European Question. It was about what Europe is and what it wants to be.

Tragically, Europe worked out its identity as a continent, its ideologies, and its loyalties, on the back and ultimately, on the ashes, of the Jews, nearly destroying the entire European civilization in the process.

When Europe is experiencing yet again rising tides of hatred and intolerance towards Jews – whatever else it might call it and however it might seek to mask it – it is time for Europe to ask what is wrong with Europe and not what is wrong with the Jews. Europe's vision of itself is challenged from within and without, and this time around, it seems that many Jews don't plan to stick around to find out how Europe will resolve the European Question "this time around."

The Arab world is no different with respect to the "Jewish Question." It is not about the Jews, and not even about Israel and Zionism, it is about the question of Arab and Muslim identity. And, like Europe before it and, sadly perhaps still today, it is working out its identity, ideologies, and loyalties – initially on the back of the Jews and now on the back of what first and foremost an ideology of activism. It was a rebellion against Jewish passivity in exile, a rejection of the Jews' resigned attitude toward their fate as a persecuted and marginalized minority. As a secular movement, it rebelled against simply waiting for the Messiah. It called for the Jewish people to be their own Messiah, to go by themselves to the Holy Land to restore Jewish sovereignty, rather than waiting for God's anointed to do it for them.

In addition, Zionism contained an element that called for the total negation of Jewish life in exile. This, however, was not true for all

Zionist thinkers. Herzl, for example, imagined that the re-establishment of Jewish sovereignty would also contribute to the life of Jews in exile by relieving them from the status of a stateless people at the mercy of the nations. He described in his novel Altneuland ("Old-New Land") that with the establishment of the Jewish state, "Jews who wished to assimilate with other peoples now felt free to do so openly, without cowardice or deception. There were also some who wished to adopt the majority religion, and these could now do so without being suspected of snobbery or careerism, for it was no longer to one's advantage to abandon Judaism."

Herzl thought that Jews would be able to walk proudly as equals among the nations once they had a state, even if they did not become its citizens. But as the situation in the Diaspora became more severe and ultimately genocidal, the choice made by many Jews to remain in Europe was scorned. For many Zionists, the growing strength of their embryonic state and the growing danger faced by the Jews of Europe delegitimize life in the Diaspora.

The negation of the exile (shlilat ha'galut in Hebrew), as it became known, was not just about negating the legitimacy of Jewish life in the Diaspora, but also negating its very essence. Zionism created an entire series of opposites expressing this: Active vs. passive, strong vs. weak, proud vs. humiliated, self-sufficient vs. dependent, healthy vs. sick. Zionism came to be seen as a cure for the sickness inflicted upon Judaism by the exile.

So when the Holocaust occurred, it was an affront to Zionism's core ideology. The Jews who perished in the Holocaust represented everything that Zionism wanted to change. The victims were seen as passive, going to their deaths like "lambs to the slaughter." They were weak, dependent, and suffered the greatest possible humiliation – an industrial genocide. Whenever they rebelled, it was because they were Zionists. The Warsaw Ghetto resistance fighters, for example, became national heroes, in part because they were members of Zionist youth movements preparing to immigrate to Israel. The survivors are even worse in the Zionist perception. They were suspected simply because they had survived. Doctor Wilf explained, "the suspicion was that they must have engaged in deceitful and treacherous actions in order to do so.

The nascent State of Israel took the Holocaust survivors in and recruited them to fight for its independence. This was, again, a pragmatic inclusiveness. Israel needed them to survive. But it did not want to hear their story, and it found no place for them in the Zionist narrative. At best, they served as Exhibit A of why there could be no Jewish life in exile. They were the negative to Zionism's positive.

Beginning with the public trial of Adolf Eichmann in 1961, however, the people of Israel not only started to listen to the survivors, but to rewrite the story of Israel and Zionism accordingly. It did not happen quickly, but over the next few decades, the story of the Holocaust and its

Herzl 's own conception of Judaism was so secular and national that he felt religious Muslims, Christians, and Jews could all be Zionists. "

And she added "Citizenship due to their Jewish ancestry, many were not Jews themselves, and some were practicing Christians. Yet their immigration to Israel was considered highly valuable – even one that "saved" the country. In fact, when their status as non-Jews did become an issue – such as the burial of fallen soldiers – it was met with anger from the broader Israeli society, indicating that, for most Israelis, they belonged fully and unquestionably. "

Gur and Wilf agreed about the process and the consequences. As doctor Wilf explained

"Over recent decades, Israel has also sought to include its Druze and Bedouin communities. The initial reason was, again, pragmatic; in this case, the need for soldiers. As early as Israel's War of Independence, many Bedouin and the entire Druze community joined the Jews in fighting off the invading Arab armies. From that moment, the Druze and many Bedouin were included in the Israel Defense Forces. Since then, Druze and Bedouin military heroes have been hailed by Israeli society and media. Indeed, during the latest conflict with Hamas, a Druze senior commander became a media hero after he demanded to be sent back into the field despite severe injuries. Many Druze self-identify as not merely Israelis, but also Zionists. This is not to say that there are no problems with discrimination or other issues, but it does show that Zionism is willing to embrace those who align themselves with it, whether Jewish or non-Jewish. Indeed, it seems that Zionism only finds it difficult to include non-Jews when they embrace competing Arab or Palestinian national identities. Zionism in itself can include non-Jews in its story, so long as they do not align themselves with a hostile narrative. "

Professor Gur correctly affirmed that the current frontier of inclusion is that of ultra- Orthodox Jews and Israeli Christians. In the past, Israeli Christians by and large adopted Arab and Palestinian identities. Christians were among the most important thinkers and shapers of modern Arab and Palestinian nationalism, and often its most zealous adherents. This is due, in part, to their status as a minority among Arab Muslims. In recent years, however, as the Arab Spring revolutions have placed the lives of Middle Eastern Christians in jeopardy, Israeli Christians have begun to explore the possibility of an Israeli rather than Arab Christian identity. As Arab identity is increasingly perceived as exclusively Muslim and even openly hostile to Christians, Israeli identity has emerged as a new possibility for identification. Like the Druze and Bedouin, this is being explored through service in the IDF, as more and more voices in the Christian community look to military service as a means of engaging with "their state." In response, the IDF is taking steps to make military service more accessible. This process has only just begun and is politically controversial, but it demonstrates again that Zionism is willing and capable of integrating non-Jews who do not embrace a competing identity hostile to Zionism.

Ultra-Orthodox Jews, for their part, have had an ambivalent relationship with Zionism from the beginning. Zionism was a thoroughly modern movement that believed human beings should shape their own fate, rather than passively accept the will of God. In addition, it was composed of mostly secular and even atheist Jews who rebelled against the religious way of life. As a result, many ultra-Orthodox thinkers saw Zionism as heresy. Wilf denounce that many of us already know but many others are not willing to accept "Some extreme ultra-Orthodox sects even claimed that Zionism was an affront to God and an obstacle to redemption"

Our most extravagant dream."

In the opening of My Promised Land, Shavit echoes Klein Halevi's feeling of anxiety. He confesses that "for as long as I can remember, I remember fear. Existential fear." But then, after detailing numerous instances of existential fear from 1967 on, he also confesses, "For as long as I can remember, I remember occupation," recounting the manner in which Israel's great victory turned "my nation" into an "occupying nation."

Klein Halevi and Shavit are haunted by these reversals and extremes. They struggle to reconcile success and failure; triumph and tragedy; the pride and the shame that are Israel and Zionism

Indeed their dream is to live in peace and prosperity ,

Our most extravagant dream as a nation is to live in a land of peace and prosperity, where all citizens can coexist harmoniously regardless of their differences. This dream, however, seems to be constantly overshadowed by the realities of conflict and occupation that have plagued our nation for decades.

The fear of existential threats has been ingrained in our collective consciousness for as long as we can remember. The constant state of war and conflict has left us with a sense of unease and uncertainty about our future. The victory of the Six-Day War in 1967, which was supposed to be a moment of triumph and celebration, instead marked the beginning of a new chapter of occupation and oppression.

The occupation of Palestinian territories has been a source of shame and guilt for many Israelis, who struggle to reconcile their national identity with the injustices committed in the name of security. The dream of a Jewish homeland, where our people can live in peace and security, has been tarnished by the realities of occupation and conflict.

Despite these challenges, there is still hope for a brighter future. The voices of peace and reconciliation are growing louder, as more and more Israelis and Palestinians come together to work towards a shared vision of coexistence. The dream of a just and peaceful society, where all citizens can live with dignity and respect, is within reach if we have the courage to pursue it.

Our most extravagant dream is not just a distant fantasy, but a tangible reality that we can strive towards every day. By acknowledging the mistakes of the past and working towards a more inclusive and equitable future, we can build a society that reflects the values of justice, equality, and peace.

In conclusion, our most extravagant dream , the zionist dream , as a nation is to live in a land where peace and prosperity reign supreme. Despite the challenges and obstacles that stand in our way, we must continue to strive towards this dream with determination and perseverance. Only by working together towards a shared vision of coexistence can we truly fulfill our most extravagant dream.

". They both understand that the decade of reversals from 1967 to 1973 to 1977, and especially the trauma of 1973, "threw the Israeli psyche out of balance." They both try to restore this balance through the personal. It is as if they have given up on any possibility of intellectually explaining Israel, Zionism, and the great revolutions of modern Jewish history. To them, Zionism and Israel are life, and just as human life is better told than explained, they try to tell the story of Israel in the only way possible: Klein Halevi focuses on the stories of seven IDF paratroopers whose lives are so representative of Israel's changes and struggles that they seem too good to be true. His protagonists are the kibbutzniks Arik Achmon, Udi Adiv, Meir Ariel, and Avital Geva; as well as the religious-Zionists Yoel Bin-Nun, Yisrael Harel, and Hanan Porat. These were the paratroopers who breached the gates of the Old City to become the first citizens of a sovereign Jewish state in two thousand years to stand on the Temple Mount and touch the stones of the Wailing Wall. They are the same paratroopers who, in an act of near-insanity, dared to cross the Suez Canal during the 1973 Yom Kippur War and turned it into Israel's Stalingrad, turning the tide toward an Israeli victory.

Even though Klein Halevi himself admits that his protagonists belong to a very small and socially homogenous group – Ashkenazi men born in the 1940s – through the seven of them and their families and friends, he is able to chronicle the entire political, ideological, economic, and cultural spectrum of Israel: from Left-wing anti-Zionism to Right-wing messianic imperialism, high-flying capitalism to spartan socialism, militant atheism to religious dogmatism, Tel Aviv hedonism to yeshiva asceticism, avant-garde conceptual art to mystical Jewish poetry. He tells the tale of their ideological battles and their fraternity in war, of that which drove them apart and later brought them back together.

From the beginning, the success rolled their eyes. "There they go against the Zionists, using their precious Holocaust to justify their state, their power, their faults, reveling in a world guilted into silence."

There are those who believe, too many, that without the holocaust there would have been no Israel. Most of them make this assumption in good faith. The American President himself, in his June 4, 2009 Cairo speech, spoke of "the recognition that the aspiration for a Jewish homeland is rooted in a tragic history that cannot be denied."

But when so many believe that without the Holocaust there would have been no Israel, those who want Israel erased from map and memory, or isolated as an illegitimate state come to resent the Holocaust, or at least its association with Israel.

The American President wanted to make an important stand against Holocaust denial in the capital of the Arab world. He did not understand that by reaffirming the dangerous equation that the global legitimacy for Israel is rooted in the Holocaust, he fanned the motivation to engage in Holocaust denial for those who continue to believe, as they always have, that Israel is not a legitimate state.

Holocaust denial, Holocaust minimization ("6 million is an exaggerated number") Holocaust "equalization" ("there were other genocides and ethnic cleansings, the Holocaust was no different"), Holocaust reversal ("what the Nazis did to the Jews is what the Jews are doing to others"), Holocaust marginalization ("other people were also killed in the War") and Holocaust by association ("the Palestinians are the secondary victims of the Holocaust"), are all but different facets of the same effort – to rob Israel of what seems like a powerful and indisputable source of legitimacy.

The deceptively seductive canard that "the Palestinians are the secondary victims of Europe's crimes" is one of the worst of all these lies, since to the untrained ear it sounds logical. In this tale, after World War II, when it became clear that the Final Solution was not final and the Jewish survivors could not be expected or welcomed to stay in Europe the Europeans decided to "dump" the surviving Jews on unsuspecting Arabs who were living in an area that colonial Europe controlled.

This convenient solution for Europe resulted in the displacement of hundreds of thousands of Palestinians who have been homeless and occupied ever since. Ergo, the Palestinians are the secondary and still uncompensated victims of Europe's crimes against the Jews.

Israel exists not because the Europeans dumped the surviving Jews in the colonially controlled Middle East. Israel exists because the Jews willed it into existence.

As correctly Wilf affirmed "The modern state of Israel exists because the Jews who created it believed themselves to be descendants of the Israelites and Judeans who were sovereign there in ancient times and paid a high price for preserving their separate existence as a people. The modern state of Israel exists"

Israel should have been created in the 1900 , that didn't happened only because Arabs prevented that issue to occur

One of the greatest obstacles to peace, and certainly the least acknowledged, is the perpetuation of the Palestinian refugee problem and the inflation of its scale by the United Nations Relief and Works Agency (UNRWA). Whereas the actual number of Arabs who could still claim to be refugees as a result of the Arab-Israeli war of 1947-1949 is today no more than several tens of thousands, the number of those registered as refugees is reaching 5 million, with millions more claiming to have that status.

UNRWA is "THE" Problem

Since the Second World War, the UN High Commissioner for Refugees has been responsible for the welfare QQ of all refugees in the world and has assisted in their resettlement and relocation – so that nearly all of them are no longer refugees – with one exception: the Arabs from Palestine. By contrast, UNRWA (Near East Relief and Work Agency), the entity created from the 1947-1949 Arab-Israeli war, has collaborated with the Arab to handle the Arab refugees from Palestine refusal to resettle the refugees in the areas where they reside, or to relocate them to third countries. Worse, UNRWA has ensured that the refugee issue only grows larger by automatically registering descendants of the original refugees from the war as refugees themselves in perpetuity, for Palestinians, uniquely, refugeeness is an hereditary trait

Professor Gur explained that the Arab states thus presented a long term and clear future planning in line with their objectives, making clear that improving the living conditions of a few hundreds of thousands of refugees was less than the war with Zionism.

Doctor Wilf's assertion that UNRWA has been engaging in bureaucratic self-aggrandizement by inflating the numbers of those under its care raises important questions about the treatment of Palestinian refugees and their descendants. The issue of Palestinian refugee status has been a contentious one for decades, with many arguing that the descendants of the original refugees from the Arab-Israeli war should not be considered refugees at all.

One of the key arguments put forth by Doctor Wilf is that the vast majority of Palestinian refugees and their descendants are citizens of third countries, such as Jordan, or live in the territories where they were born, such as Gaza and the West Bank. This raises the question of whether these individuals truly qualify as refugees under international law. According to the United Nations High Commissioner for

Refugees (UNHCR), a refugee is someone who has been forced to flee their country due to persecution, war, or violence. However, if individuals are citizens of another country or territory, or if they are living in their country of birth and have a future there, they may not meet the criteria for refugee status.

Furthermore, the Palestinians born in the West Bank and Gaza are not fleeing war or seeking refuge – they are considered citizens of Palestine by the Palestinian Authority itself. This raises questions about why they are still classified as refugees by UNRWA. No other group of people in the world is registered as refugees while also being citizens of another country or territory. This raises concerns about the accuracy of UNRWA's refugee numbers and the potential for bureaucratic manipulation.

Additionally, if the European Union has adopted the policy that Gaza and the West Bank are territories to be allocated to Palestine, and some EU countries already recognize Palestine as a state, then it seems illogical for Palestinians living in these territories to be classified as refugees. If these territories are considered part of a future Palestinian state, then the individuals living there should be considered citizens of that state, not refugees.

In conclusion, Doctor Wilf's assertion that UNRWA has been engaging in bureaucratic self-aggrandizement by inflating the numbers of those under its care raises important questions about the treatment of Palestinian refugees and their descendants. The issue of Palestinian refugee status is a complex and contentious one, and it is crucial that it be addressed in a fair and transparent manner. If the descendants of the Arab refugees from the Arab-Israeli war do not meet the criteria for refugee status, then it is important that their status be reevaluated and that they be treated like all other refugees, including Jewish refugees.

to argue that people who were born and are living in Palestine are refugees from... Palestine.

The remaining 20 percent of the descendants who are not Jordanian citizens or citizens of the Palestinian Authority in Gaza and the West Bank, are inhabitants of Syria and Lebanon who are by law denied the right to citizenship granted to all other Syrians and Lebanese.

Doctor Inat Wilf affirmed that "Yet, UNRWA does nothing to fight for the right of these Lebanese and Syrian-born Arabs to citizenship, collaborating in their discrimination and the perpetuation of their refugee status. "

Professor Aviv Gur explained why this matters for peace. Because if millions of Arabs who are citizens of Jordan and the Palestinian Authority, or inhabitants of Syria and Lebanon, claim to be refugees from what is today Israel, even though they were never born there and never lived there, and demand that as a result of this refugee status they are given the right to relocate to Israel ('the right of return'), then the whole basis for peace by means of two states for two people crumbles. Wilf also explained correctly the fact that if Israel with its 6 million Jews and more than 1.5 million Arabs has to absorb between 5 and 8 million Palestinians, then the Jews will be relegated again to living as a minority among those who do not view them as able to exercise their right to self- determination would be no more.

Western Complicity

UN WATCH is a real significant and relevant institution . Its contribution to the fight against antisemitism is something really important. In a report it explained it very clearly .Arguing that it is even more absurd is that UNRWA is funded by countries who support two states for two peoples. The United States, the EU, Canada, Japan and Australia fund 99 per cent of UNRWA's annual budget of over $1 billion, whereas the 56 Islamic countries who supposedly grieve for their Palestinian brethren supply only a few million dollars.

Un watch also using some , "if the policy of Western countries towards the Jewish settlements in the West Bank were to take its cue from their policy towards the Palestinian refugees as shaped by UNRWA, it would go as follows: 'Go ahead Israel, build as many settlements as you want and keep expanding them in perpetuity. We will accept the settlements as a natural expansion of Israel. We will even support the expansion effort financially. Don't tell the settlers that they will ever need to leave their homes, teach them that it is their legal right to be there. We trust that when the day comes to negotiate peace with the Arab world you will do so in good faith and in a way that guarantees the existence of a sovereign and contiguous Arab state in Gaza and the West Bank."

And they remarks "it stands right now the policy of Western countries towards UNRWA is precisely that – it is essentially telling the Arab world: 'Go ahead and keep inflating the numbers of refugees in perpetuity by registering as descendants of refugees and as refugees themselves. Register them as refugees from Palestine even though they were born and are living in the Palestinian Authority.".

"Allow them to maintain both a refugee status and citizenship from a third country. Keep telling them that even though they were born in Gaza and Ramallah, they are actually from Ashdod and Ashkelon and can realistically expect to live there soon. Keep them in a discriminated-against state in Syria and Lebanon, where their basic human rights are denied, just so they can keep the conflict alive. We trust that when the day comes to negotiate a final settlement with Israel, you will do so in good faith in a way that guarantees the coherence and existence of a Jewish state."

Dr Einat Wilf go deeper

"If the first policy appears preposterous to Western governments who support peace by means of a two-state solution, then so should the second. If Western countries truly want to remove obstacles on the road to peace, they cannot condemn the growth of settlements on one hand and condone the manufactured growth of the number of refugees on the other. Either both the growth of settlements and the inflation in the number of refugees should be treated as obstacles to peace, or neither should be. Moreover, whereas Israel has demonstrated time and again that for peace with Egypt – and for much less than peace in Gaza and the northern West Bank – it will ruthlessly and effectively uproot settlements, the Palestinians have yet to demonstrate that they are willing to take even the smallest steps to give the palestinian refugee problem a solution, but that UNRWA had indeed been turn in a political instrument for the perpetuation of the problem. These people were none other than the agency's own chiefs, who had repeatedly warned it throughout the 1950s that Unrwa had reached deadlock, its activity and even its existence needing reevaluation. "

And she added

"As early as their 1953 report , UNRWA chiefs suggested scalping back the agency's work and transferring operational responsibility for the refugees to the Arab states.

Throughout the world, in the 1940 and the 1950, millions of refugees were rehabilitated in the country's that had given then shelter ; 600.00 Chinese find shelter in British Hong Kong, nearly a million of refugees from North Vietnam where rehabilitated in South Vietnam, some fourteen million Hindu and Muslim refugees find shelter in India and Pakistan, respectively, following the partition of the Indian subcontinent in 1947, more than ten million ethnic germans and savagely expelled from Eastern Europe log after WWII was over ang Germany surrendered, found shelter in West Germany, and the young and impoverished state of Israel took it upon itself to absorb hundreds of thousands of jewish refugees-orphans, widows, men who had lost their families in the Nazi death Camps as well as jews from Arab countries who were forced out of thor homes with the clothes they were wearing. "

Doctor Wilf remarks "ts is clear UNRWA's birth which saw economic rehabilitation and

resettlement of the refugees as the only realistic way to end the problem on the one hand ; while on the other hand, the Arabs were striving to perpetuate

the problem by maintaining an ever-increasing roster of Palestinian"refugees"

and keeping the hope of return alive and very present."

Doctor Wilf explains "recognition of the State of Palestine Conflict with its support for a United Nations Refugee organization that it backs to the tune of tens of millions of dollars per year. "

The original sin in introducing the idea of a Palestinian "right to return" was committed not by an Arab politician, but by a Swedish Count, Folke Bernadotte. Bernadotte, a member of the Swedish royal family, was appointed as the UN mediator in the Arab-Israeli conflict shortly after Israel's establishment. His mission was to mediate between the sides and end the war that had erupted in the region.

Before his appointment as the UN mediator, Bernadotte had a distinguished career as the deputy head of the Swedish Red Cross during the Second World War. He became the president of the organization in 1946 and played a crucial role in negotiating the release of thousands of Scandinavian prisoners, including a few hundred Jews, from Nazi Germany. This act of heroism initially helped allay Israeli concerns over Bernadotte's appointment as the UN mediator.

However, the chief obstacle in Bernadotte's mission was the approach of the Arab world, which vehemently opposed recognizing the state of Israel in any borders whatsoever. As Einat Wiif points out, this opposition created a significant challenge for Bernadotte in his efforts to mediate a peaceful resolution to the conflict.

It was during his mediation efforts that Bernadotte introduced the idea of a Palestinian "right to return." This concept, which asserts that Palestinian refugees have the right to return to their homes in Israel, has been a contentious issue in the Israeli-Palestinian conflict ever since. The introduction of this idea by Bernadotte marked a turning point in the conflict and has had far-reaching implications for the peace process in the region.

In conclusion, the original sin in introducing the idea of a Palestinian "right to return" was committed by Folke Bernadotte, a Swedish Count and UN mediator in the Arab-Israeli conflict. Despite his noble intentions and heroic actions during the Second World War, Bernadotte's introduction of this concept has had lasting consequences for the peace process in the Middle East. It serves as a reminder of the complexities and challenges inherent in resolving the Israeli-Palestinian conflict.

His attempts to secure a compromise were first a matter only of politics, given the web of interests and the desires of the great powers at the time.On the one hand, Britain and the United States sought to preserve Western hegemony in the Middle East in order to prevent Soviet penetration and guarantee the continuous flow of oil from the Levant to Europe and questioned other similar matters. On the other hand, the Soviet Union sought to undermine Western control in the region by subverting those same pro-British monarchical regimes.The question of geopolitical power- not justice and morality- as Einat Wilf explains, was the factor that mostly influenced Bernadotte´s activities. What Bernadotte did, as representative of the Western Power, was to grant a seal of approval to the Arab ambition to eliminate the state of Israel.

Bernadotte's approach greatly diverged from the generally accepted way of dealing with refugee problems at the time , and remains into the present day one of the biggest obstacles to achieving a peace deal.

Like many foreign envoys who followed Bernadotte through the decades, Bernadotte accepted the Arab objection to Zionism as an immutable fact of nature, seeking neither to challenge nor change it.He therefore persisted in what appeared as the easier path of trying to chip away at Israel sovereignty by pressuring Israel to do even more concessions.

Bernadotte's conversations in Tel-Aviv with the Israeli leadership took place in a completely different spirit. While thousands of Jews were still in displaced persons camps in Europe and Cyprus, trying to recover from the horrors of the Holocaust, and while their compatriots were fighting to achieve sovereignty in a fraction of a percentage Middle East, Bernardotte thought it right to lecture Moshe Sharet about how to win the hearts of the world. Meating the Israeli minister, the Swedish mediator accused the Israeli of"arrogance and hostility"saying that what matters most for the Jews was to increase their good- will in the world at large and that Jews "ought to set themselves forth with to counteract the prevailing hatred between Arabs and jews". If the Israeli government had acted differently, he argued,"its prestige in the world at large would have been immeasurably increased".

Like many foreign envoys who followed Bernadotte throughout decades, Bernadette accepted the Arab objections to Zionism as an immutable fact of nature, seeking neither to change nor to challenge them. He persisted in an easy path of trying to pressure Israel to make more concessions.

As Bernadotte continued his efforts to service the interests of the great powers and realizing that his only path to appeasing the Arabs, was to pressure Israel as much as possible.

He set a number of precedents regarding the Arab refugees, which would continue to fuel the Arab Israeli conflict. He was the first to decide that responsibility for the stateless Palestinian refugees should fall in the international community via the United Nations: the Arabs were inhabitants of the territory entrusted by the international community to Britain as a mandate, Bernadotte thought, so they understandably expected tangible assistance from the United Nations.In that, Bernadotte overlooked the Palestinians Arab's own responsibility for their fate and their choice not to establish in their own state as offered by the international community, which would have given territory, citizenship and statehood.

Bernadotte also demanded the return of the Arab refugees to the territory of the state of Israel. Bernadotte's position was exceptional, first in his insistence on the return of the refugee population against the wishes of the sovereign state, and also ignoring the real danger of perpetuating the war (in contradiction to his role as a peacemaker or mediator).

The UNRWA – the United Nations Relief and Works Agency, which provides social and welfare services to the original Palestinian refugees from the 1947-1949 Arab–Jewish war.

UNRWA took quite a bit of heat for a Hamas tunnel found beneath one of its facilities during the Gaza war this summer, and for turning over rockets found at one of its facilities to Hamas "authorities." But that pales in comparison to the scorn it has earned for its policy of recognizing the descendants of the original refugees – a policy that has led to the mushrooming of refugee figures from 800,000 in 1949 to more than 5 million today.

Indeed, UNRWA has effectively perpetuated the refugee problem, making any amelioration or resolution of their situation that does not involve the demand to "return to Palestine" virtually impossible.

The issue of Palestine and the recognition of its statehood has been a contentious and complex issue in international politics for decades.

The criteria of international law, as mentioned in the prompt, clearly shows that there is already one Palestinian state and it is Jordan . Nevertheless, it could be considered another state. It has a defined territory, a people, and a government. The territory in question if it will be relevant could be the West Bank and Gaza, as defined by the pre-1967 cease-fire lines.

However, the situation becomes more complicated when considering the status of Palestinian refugees living in these territories. Sweden, for example, recognizes the State of Palestine, yet there are still an estimated two million Palestinian refugees living in the West Bank and Gaza. These refugees are registered as "refugees from Palestine," even though they are technically living within the borders of the recognized state of Palestine. This raises the question of how these refugees can continue to be classified as such if a state already exists to which they claim to belong.

This dilemma highlights a fundamental contradiction in the policies of those who support organizations like UNRWA, which provide assistance to Palestinian refugees. UNRWA operates under the premise that there is a distinct Palestinian identity and territory, yet the existence of a recognized state of Palestine complicates this narrative. The idea of a Palestinian state has long been a central goal for the Palestinian people, but the reality of its existence raises questions about the continued status of Palestinian refugees.

The issue of Palestinian statehood is further complicated by the historical and political context of the region. The conflict between Israel and Palestine has been ongoing for decades, with both sides claiming the same territory as their own. The recognition of Palestine as a state by some countries, like Sweden, is seen as a step towards a resolution of the conflict. However, the status of Palestinian refugees remains a significant obstacle to achieving a lasting peace.

In conclusion, the recognition of Palestine as a state by countries like Sweden is a positive step towards resolving the Israeli-Palestinian conflict. However, the continued status of Palestinian refugees living within the borders of the recognized state of Palestine raises important questions about the future of the Palestinian people. It is clear that a comprehensive and inclusive solution is needed to address the needs and aspirations of all Palestinians, both within and outside the borders of a recognized Palestinian state.

The first related to the end of Jewish sovereignty over the land, and the second related to its prospective renewal.

The Roman Emperor Hadrian was the first to make official use of the name 'Palestine' or 'Palestine' to refer to the region between the Jordan River and the Mediterranean. To secure the end of Jewish resistance to the Roman Empire he not only quashed their revolt and forced them into exile, but he dismantled the Province of Judea, as it was called at the time, and renamed it Palestina. This name was taken from the writings of the Greek historian Herodotus, referring to the Biblical and Egyptian 'Pleshet' or land of the 'Philistines' on the southern coast (near present day Gaza). During the following centuries of Arab and Ottoman domination of the region it was no longer called Palestine but the southern part of 'Al-Sham,' or greater Syria (the territory claimed now by the Islamic State).

The only other political entity in the Middle East to bear the name Palestine was the British Mandate, constituted in 1920 by the League of Nations, for the express purpose of effecting 'the establishment in Palestine of a national home for the Jewish people.' The mandate allowed Britain the option of cutting the territory east of the River Jordan out of the mandate for a Jewish national home, which it duly exercised two years later, with the creation of Transjordan, today's Jordan. This step actually further serves to emphasize the connection between the name Palestine and the project of Jewish national liberation in the historic homeland of the Jewish people: land which was now closed to Jewish settlement no longer bore the name Palestine, and Palestine itself had – from that point in 1922 until the end of the mandate in 1948 – the borders that today encompass Israel, the West Bank, and the Gaza Stip. These borders are often referred to as 'historic Palestine.' Usually without mentioning that they are 'historic' only insofar as they lasted for barely three decades, were governed by a European superpower, and delimited as the future national home for the Jewish people.

In the years of the mandate, both Jews and Arabs in Palestine were referred to as Palestinians. There was a mass-circulation Arab daily called Falastin and a popular Jewish one called The Palestine Post. Jewish organizations as diverse as the Philharmonic and the fledgling Football League had the word Palestine in their names too.

One of the most vocal critics of UNRWA is Einat Wilf, an Israeli politician and former member of the Knesset. In a statement made at the United Nations, Wilf argued that UNRWA has failed to fulfill its mandate of providing humanitarian assistance to Palestinian refugees and has instead perpetuated the conflict in the region.

Wilf pointed out that UNRWA is the only UN agency dedicated to a specific group of refugees, the Palestinians, while all other refugees around the world are served by the United Nations High Commissioner for Refugees (UNHCR). This special treatment, according to Wilf, has allowed UNRWA to maintain the refugee status of Palestinians for generations, creating a cycle of dependency and victimhood that has hindered the prospects for peace in the region.

Furthermore, Wilf criticized UNRWA for its ties to Hamas, the terrorist organization that governs the Gaza Strip. She argued that UNRWA schools and facilities have been used by Hamas to store weapons and launch attacks against Israel, putting the lives of Palestinian civilians at risk. By turning a blind eye to these activities, UNRWA has effectively become complicit in terrorism and has undermined its own credibility as a humanitarian organization.

Wilf also highlighted the financial mismanagement and corruption within UNRWA, pointing to reports of employees engaging in nepotism and embezzlement of funds. She argued that this mismanagement has diverted resources away from the refugees who are in desperate need of assistance, further exacerbating their suffering.

In conclusion, Einat Wilf's declaration at the United Nations sheds light on the problematic role that UNRWA has played in the Palestinian refugee crisis. By perpetuating the refugee status of Palestinians, maintaining ties to terrorist organizations, and engaging in financial mismanagement, UNRWA has failed to fulfill its mandate and has instead contributed to the perpetuation of conflict in the region. It is clear that reforms are needed within UNRWA in order to truly address the needs of Palestinian refugees and work towards a lasting peace in the Middle East.

However, Arab refugees who fled during the 1948 War of Independence refused to be resettled because they believed it meant recognition of the State of Israel. Despite the initial failure, Arab countries pressured the West not to close UNRWA because they wanted to keep it "a permanent question mark on the existence of the Jewish state," Wilf explains. UNRWA has trained generations of people who feel compelled to "liberate Palestine" and reclaim the "lost paradise." This education, through the refugee status itself and the school program, "naturally generates terrorist organizations," says Wilf. "Hamas is a product of today's UNRWA, just as those who carried out the massacre of Israeli athletes in Munich in 1972 were also children of those camps, they were also a product of UNRWA schools." "We have more than two million people here who believe they were born in Palestine but who are still registered as Palestine refugees. Which is Palestine? The one that will be liberated and will replace the Jewish State. Wilf argues that these two million people would not be considered refugees under any other international standard. Another 40% of the registered refugees are Jordanian citizens, he explained, and many of them have reached the upper middle class and are businessmen, merchants, etc. Most of them no longer live in "refugee" camps.

Approximately one million people lived in Lebanon and Syria. Many of them left those countries in recent years and moved to Europe, but even if they obtained citizenship in their new country, they remain on UNRWA records. Because UNRWA automatically registers the next generation as refugees, the UNRWA card has essentially become a marker of Palestinian identity, Wilf explained, and the services it provides primarily serve as a pretext for UNRWA's continued existence. According to Wilf, UNRWA currently has two main objectives: "The first is to keep the Jewish State in the air until the return occurs. The end of Israel is the only thing that will end the refugee status. So it is an organization that perpetuates the conflict from generation to generation until the Jews no longer have a state." Writer and former Knesset member Einat Wilf claims that UNRWA has perpetuated the falsehood that Palestinians remain refugees from a conflict that ended 76 years ago to push the idea of the right of return in an attempt to undermine the validity of the Jewish state. . He believes that UNRWA should only help those who are no longer considered refugees and do not claim the right of return.

Professor Gur affirmed UNRWA has many problems but according to Gur, its perpetuation of the Palestinian refugee crisis their most complicated contribution to the conflict

UNRWA was established in 1949 to provide assistance to Palestinian refugees who were displaced during the Arab-Israeli conflict. However, unlike other refugee agencies, UNRWA defines refugees not only as those who were displaced themselves, but also their descendants. This unique definition has led to the perpetuation of the refugee crisis, as the number of registered refugees has grown exponentially over the years.

Gur argues that this perpetuation of the refugee crisis serves a political purpose, as it keeps the Palestinian issue at the forefront of the international agenda. By maintaining a large population of refugees, UNRWA ensures that the Palestinian cause remains relevant and garners international sympathy and support

También sostiene que los palestinos tienen la capacidad de mejorar su situación, pero han optado por priorizar la destrucción del Estado judío.

La Dra. Einat Wilf explica la esencia de UNRWA en una reunión informativa para delegaciones de la ONU en la sede de la ONU en Nueva York, organizada por el Embajador de Israel ante la ONU.

Este informe ofrece un resumen de la historia de la UNRWA y de cómo se convirtió en la columna vertebral ideológica de la visión palestina del "retorno" violento manifestada el 7 de octubre, y de cómo la UNRWA ha dado origen a todas las organizaciones terroristas, desde Septiembre Negro hasta Hamás.

What are the arguments for and against continuing support for UNRWA?

Against: Unlike UNHCR's mandate — to settle the refugees. UNRWA's mandate is to prevent Arab refugees who, as the result of their attack on Israel, left/were expelled, from integrating/wanting to integrate into other societies — to keep them and their descendants, refugees.

For: It provides for refugees — food, clothes, activities. Which, if you keep the people from working, needs to be done. Nobody wants a humanitarian crisis.

In short — like a Russian ditty about ambulances — by itself it tramples pedestrians, by itself it takes care of them. UNRWA takes care of the possible problem

Why does the UN have a separate organization for Palestinian refugees (UNRWA)?

UNRWA was established on 8 December, 1949 to deal with the needs of the Arab refugees from the 1948–49 Arab-Israeli war and maintain them until their return to their homes in the former Palestine. The Arab rejection of UNGAR 194 due to its "implied recognition of Israel" in the condition that direct negotiations between the parties would determine international borders and the terms of a permanent peace replacing the 1949 Rhodes Armistice Agreements.

The following year, the United Nations High Commissioner for Refugees was established (14 December, 1950), with a

Former Armored Recon Platoon Sgt., 188th Armored (ret.) at Israel Defense Forces

What are the arguments for and against continuing support for UNRWA?

UNRWA is a "temporary" UN agency that was designed to maintain the health, education and welfare of Arab refugees from the War of Independence, until they "could be returned to their homes and live in peace with their neighbors" as described in UNGAR 194. The only real problem with that is that the Arabs, in toto, rejected UNGAR 194 in its entirety.

By the mid-1950s, it should have become clear that this was not a job for a temporary agency, especially after the establishment of the UNHCR, which cares for refugees from the rest of the world. The Arab League

What is UNRWA, and what does it do for Palestinians?

Let's see how it works. During the 1948 Palestine War, which was started by 5 Arab states to destroy Israel, around 700,000 Palestinian Arabs fled from their homes. In 1949, the UNRWA defined them as

Palestinian refugees as well as their patrilineal descendants. Thus they are the only refugees in the world who inherit their status. Being a Palestinian refugee had become a family business. UNRWA pays them for being refugees. It provides them with food and housing. Instead of solving the refugees problem, this totally corrupted and absolutely useless structure has multiplied their amount from 700

What is the significance of UN Secretary-General Antonio Guterres' statement on UNRWA's future and its impact on Palestine refugees?

If the UN wanted to resolve the issue it would demand that Jordan receive the Refugees.

Jordan got around 75% of British Palestine whilst Israel go

What issues or controversies surround UNRWA?

Israel revealed that six UNRWA workers were part of the wave of terrorists who breached the Gaza-Israel border and massacred civilians inside of ...

UNRWA, the UN body that provides welfare and humanitarian services for Palestinian refugees from the 1948 and 1967 wars and their descendants, is itself currently under Relate Is the UN's lead agency for assisting Palestinians, UNRWA, fatally compromised by its operations in Gaza?

For sure, Hamas and other radical Islamists are documents that indicate that the same offices were also used by Hamas. (Times of Israel[1], February 11, 2024; @IDFSpokesperson[2], February 10, 2024). Ten days earlier, The Wall Street Journal[3] had reported: "In 2014, part of the parking lot at the Unrwa headquarters in Gaza began sinking, likely from a Hamas tunnel dug beneath. 'No one talked about what

---

1.   https://www.timesofisrael.com/directly-beneath-unrwas-gaza-headquarters-idf-uncovers-top-secret-hamas-data-center/

2.   https://twitter.com/IDFSpokesperson/status/1756378313386254457

3.   https://www.wsj.com/world/middle-east/hamas-israel-attack-united-nations-unrwa-0ec8d325

was causing the collapse,' a former Unrwa official said, "but everyone knew.'"

.

Furthermore, UNRWA's collaboration with Hamas, as evidenced by the cables discovered by the IDF, raises serious concerns about the organization's neutrality and impartiality. Hamas, a recognized terrorist group, has been known to use humanitarian aid as a cover for its terrorist activities. By allowing Hamas to operate within its premises, UNRWA is complicit in supporting terrorism and undermining peace efforts in the region.

Gur argues that the international community must address the root cause of the Palestinian refugee crisis by pushing for a resolution to the Israeli-Palestinian conflict. This includes finding a just and lasting solution for the Palestinian refugees, rather than perpetuating their status as eternal refugees.

In conclusion, Haviv Rettig Gur's analysis of UNRWA's problem sheds light on the complexities of the Palestinian refugee crisis. While the presence of terrorists within UNRWA is a serious concern, the organization's perpetuation of the refugee crisis and collaboration with Hamas are even more troubling.

Professor Gur remarks "it is imperative that the international community address these issues and work towards a resolution that upholds the rights and dignity of all those affected by the conflict."

Aviv Gur denounced clearly the sinister role of UNRWA, he affirmed that "Promoting hate and indoctrination of antisemitism is a dangerous and destructive practice that has far-reaching consequences. Antisemitism, or hatred and discrimination against Jewish people, has a long and troubling history that continues to manifest itself in various forms today. One of the key players in perpetuating this hate speech is the United Nations Relief and Works Agency for Palestine Refugees in the Near East (UNRWA).

UNRWA was established in 1949 to provide assistance and support to Palestinian refugees in the Middle East. While its mission is noble and important, there have been numerous reports and allegations of the agency promoting hate speech and antisemitism. This is particularly concerning given that UNRWA receives significant funding from various countries and organizations, including the United States.

One of the ways in which UNRWA has been accused of promoting hate speech is through its educational materials and curriculum. Reports have shown that textbooks used in UNRWA schools contain anti-Israel and antisemitic content, including glorification of violence and martyrdom. This indoctrination of hate at a young age can have lasting effects on the attitudes and beliefs of Palestinian children, perpetuating a cycle of hatred and conflict.

Furthermore, UNRWA has been criticized for employing individuals with ties to terrorist organizations, further perpetuating a culture of hate and violence. By allowing individuals with extremist views to work within the agency, UNRWA is sending a dangerous message that violence and hatred are acceptable means of achieving political goals."

In addition to UNRWA's role in promoting hate speech, Arab leaders in the region have also played a significant role in perpetuating antisemitism. From inflammatory rhetoric to denying the Holocaust, Arab leaders have used their platforms to spread hateful and discriminatory views towards Jewish people. This kind of rhetoric only serves to further fuel tensions and perpetuate a cycle of violence and hatred.

Promoting hate and indoctrination of antisemitism

The antisemitism promotion is a dangerous and destructive practice that must be addressed and condemned. UNRWA, as a key player in the region, must take responsibility for its role in perpetuating hate speech and work towards promoting peace and understanding.

Arab leaders must also be held accountable for their inflammatory rhetoric and discriminatory views. Only through education, dialogue, and mutual respect can we hope to overcome the cycle of hatred and violence that has plagued the region for far too long.

1. UNRWA aid used by Hamas. Bags of UNRWA labeled concrete found in tunnels used by Hamas to hold hostages (shown in video clip at 4:50 and 7:10) (Economic Times YouTube[4], February 8, 2024).

2. At least 12 UNRWA staff participated on October 7. Israeli intelligence found evidence that at least 12 UNRWA employees participated in the October 7th attack, including six that took part in the invasion, two that held hostages, and others that transported ammunition (The Wall Street Journal[5], January 29, 2024; New York Times[6], January 28, 2024). On February 16th, Israeli Defense Minister Yoav Gallant announced the identity of all 12 of these UNRWA employees, including Faisal Ali Mussalem al-Naami, an UNRWA social worker, seen in a surveillance video from October 7th abducting the body of an Israeli killed in the attack (Times of Israel[7], February 16th, 2024).

3. Hamas shot at IDF troops from UNRWA school. An injured IDF soldier testified that he was injured when Hamas fighters shot at him from an UNRWA school, killing his commander. According to the injured soldier, the Hamas fighters used the

---

4. https://www.youtube.com/watch?v=BfsvO88g_B0

5. https://www.wsj.com/world/middle-east/at-least-12-u-n-agency-employees-involved-in-oct-7-attacks-intelligence-reports-say-a7de8f36

6. https://www.nytimes.com/2024/01/28/world/middleeast/gaza-unrwa-hamas-israel.html

7. https://www.timesofisrael.com/video-shows-unrwa-social-worker-abducting-body-of-israeli-on-oct-7/

school as cover to attack Israeli troops and also to store weapons. (@ChayaRaichik10[8], January 30, 2024).

4. 1,200 UNRWA employees are Hamas and PIJ operatives. Israeli intelligence estimated that 10% of UNRWA's Gaza workforce, equaling 1,200 UNRWA employees, are Hamas and Palestinian Islamic Jihad operatives while 50% or 6,000 UNRWA employees have immediate family members who are affiliated with these terror groups. (The Wall Street Journal[9], January 29, 2024).

5. UNRWA facilities used for Hamas weapons storage. Col. Elad Shushan, commander of the 646th Reserve Paratroopers Brigade: "There is not a UNRWA site, school, mosque, or kindergarten in which we didn't find weapons. None. One hundred percent." (Times of Israel[10], January 18, 2024).

6. UNRWA aid stolen by Hamas. In a recorded call with Israel, a Gaza resident who works for an American aid organization testified that Hamas systematically steals equipment and food, including stealing from UNRWA warehouses. (@cogatonline[11], January 8, 2024).

7. UNRWA aid bags used by Hamas to store equipment. Photo shows Nukhba military vests found in UNRWA bags inside a medical clinic. (@cogatonline[12], January 6, 2024).

8. Hamas Controls UNRWA. Gaza Palestinian tells IDF in recorded phone call that Hamas controls UNRWA and is hoarding all the supplies. "Hamas has their hands on

---

8. https://twitter.com/ChayaRaichik10/status/1752114182391058811

9. https://www.wsj.com/world/middle-east/at-least-12-u-n-agency-employees-involved-in-oct-7-attacks-intelligence-reports-say-a7de8f36

10. https://www.timesofisrael.com/in-central-gaza-where-gunmen-lurk-underground-a-commander-sees-a-long-slog-ahead/

11. https://twitter.com/cogatonline/status/1744366954167533829

12. https://twitter.com/cogatonline/status/1743570061363642836

UNRWA administration workers, and it manages UNRWA, from the day they [Hamas] rose to power they took control of everything."(New York Post[13], December 25, 2023).

9. UN equipment used by Hamas. UN vests were found together with ammunition and explosives, some inside UNRWA aid bags. (@IDF[14], December 25, 2023).

10. Vehicles and machines stolen from UNRWA facility. According to a social media user in Gaza, vehicles and heavy machinery were stolen from an UNRWA facility (@JoeTruzman[15], December 25, 2023).

11. UNRWA aid bags used to store weapons. IDF video shows explosives, a Kalashnikov rifle, and an RPG that had been found stored in UNRWA aid bags. (IDF Website[16], December 11, 2023).

12. UNRWA aid bags used to store weapons. Photos and video show Hamas weapons found UNRWA aid bags inside a mosque in Shuja'iyya. (@cogatonline[17], Dec. 11, 2023; @JoeTruzman[18], December 11, 2024).

---

13. https://nypost.com/2023/12/25/news/hamas-in-control-of-unrwa-aid-group-in-gaza-palestinian-man/

14. https://twitter.com/IDF/status/1739307482608984088

15. https://twitter.com/JoeTruzman/status/1739077698650333223

16. https://www.idf.il/en/mini-sites/hamas-israel-war-24/war-on-hamas-2023-resources/ammunition-found-inside-unrwa-bags/#_853ae90f0351324bd73ea615e6487517__4c761f170e016836ff84498202b99827__853ae90f0351324bd73ea615e6487517_text_43ec3e5dee6e706af7766fffea512721_During_0bcef9c45bd8a48eda1b26eb0c61c869_20an_0bcef9c45bd8a48eda1b26eb0c61c869_20operation_0bcef9c45bd8a48eda1b26eb0c61c869_20In_0bcef9c45bd8a48eda1b26eb0c61c869_20the_c0cb5f0fcf239ab3d9c1fcd31fff1efc_of_0bcef9c45bd8a48eda1b26eb0c61c869_20civilians_0bcef9c45bd8a48eda1b26eb0c61c869_20for_0bcef9c45bd8a48eda1b26eb0c61c869_20terror_0bcef9c45bd8a48eda1b26eb0c61c869_20purposes

17. https://twitter.com/cogatonline/status/1734272381466652853

13. UNRWA school was used as a base to fire weapons. An IDF video shows Hamas terrorists firing weapons from inside an UNRWA school in Beit Hanoun. (@IDF[19], December 9, 2023).

14. UNRWA aid bags used to store weapons. Video shows weapons found in a school which had been stored in UNRWA aid bags. (@IDFSpokesperson[20], December 9, 2023).

15. Hamas fires rockets from near a UN facility. Satellite photo shows site from where Hamas launched 12 rockets at Israeli civilians. Site is in close proximity to a UN facility. (@cogatonline[21], December 7, 2023).

16. Armas ocultas bajo el equipamiento de la UNRWA. Las fuerzas de las FDI encontraron decenas de misiles y cohetes Grad ocultos debajo del equipamiento de la UNRWA. (Jerusalem Post[22] , 2 de diciembre de 2023; @JoeTruzman[23] , 2 de diciembre de 2023; @IDFSpokesperson[24] , 2 de diciembre de 2023).

17. Hamás roba ayuda de la UNRWA. Un vídeo muestra bolsas de ayuda de la UNRWA dentro del túnel terrorista de Hamás. (@cogatonline[25] , 30 de noviembre de 2023).

18. Un profesor de la UNRWA mantiene como rehén a un israelí. Un israelí que regresó como prisionero testificó que un profesor de la UNRWA lo mantuvo cautivo en un ático

18. https://twitter.com/JoeTruzman/status/1734256276459397410

19. https://twitter.com/IDF/status/1733419795821871319

20. https://twitter.com/IDFSpokesperson/status/1733450024703475802

21. https://twitter.com/cogatonline/status/1732691140493615547

22. https://www.jpost.com/arab-israeli-conflict/gaza-news/article-776170

23. https://twitter.com/JoeTruzman/status/1731004268482863383

24. https://twitter.com/IDFSpokesperson/status/1730927776159449142

25. https://twitter.com/cogatonline/status/1730250928861721029

durante 50 días. (@bokeralmog[26] , 29 de noviembre de 2023).

19. Túnel terrorista de Hamás ubicado cerca de una escuela de la UNRWA. El 8 de noviembre de 2023, las FDI destruyeron un túnel terrorista de Hamás que se encontraba junto a una escuela de la UNRWA. (FDD[27] , 10 de noviembre de 2023; @JoeTruzman[28] , 8 de noviembre de 2023; @IDF[29] , 3 de diciembre de 2023).

20. Hamás lanza cohetes desde cerca de las instalaciones de la ONU. La imagen satelital muestra el sitio de lanzamiento de cohetes de Hamás junto al edificio de la ONU. (@IDF[30] , 22 de octubre de 2023).

21. Hamás lanza cohetes desde las inmediaciones de una instalación de la ONU. La imagen satelital muestra el sitio de lanzamiento de cohetes de Hamás junto a la escuela de la UNRWA. (@cogatonline[31] , 19 de octubre de 2023).

22. Hamás roba combustible de la UNRWA. El Ministerio de Salud de Hamás robó 24.000 litros de combustible de una instalación de la UNRWA

The insidious and horrible role of UNRWA

The general secretary of the United Nations , Mr Guterrez affirm that

Hamas Attacks Did Not Happen in A Vacuum: And he was right but in a total opposite way that he was thinking about

26. https://twitter.com/bokeralmog/status/1729934849161494658

27. https://www.fdd.org/analysis/2023/11/10/hamas-terror-tunnel-next-to-unrwa-school-in-gaza-destroyed/

28. https://twitter.com/JoeTruzman/status/1722302546222674067

29. https://twitter.com/IDF/status/1731071286753771620

30. https://twitter.com/IDF/status/1716156227585974585

31. https://twitter.com/cogatonline/status/1714940859030933813

The UNRWA Teachers

We hear clearly the following: on October 24th, United Nations Secretary-General Antonio Guterres stated that the Hamas massacre of October 7th "did not happen in a vacuum." He was right. The attacks were perpetrated by Palestinians who for generations were indoctrinated with hatred.

As we have shown in numerous reports over the past decade, teachers and schools at the United Nations Relief and Works Agency, which runs education and social services for Palestinians, regularly call to murder Jews, and create teaching materials that glorify terrorism, encourage martyrdom, demonize Israelis and incite anti semitism.

UN watch for example, reported how in May 2022, UNRWA teacher Elham Mansour, posted this on Facebook: "By Allah, anyone who can kill and slaughter any Zionist and Israel criminal, and doesn't do so, doesn't deserve to live. Kill them and pursue them everywhere, they are the greatest enemy. All Israel deserves is death."

This is how Palestinians in Gaza and elsewhere were educated in UNRWA schools, and that is exactly what the Hamas murderers and rapists did on October 7 th .

In 2022 alone, UNRWA received $344 million in U.S. funding. Yet a March 2023 report by UN Watch and Impact-SE identified 133 UNRWA educators and staff who were found to promote hate and violence on social media, and an additional 82 teachers and other staff affiliated with 30 UNRWA schools who were involved in drafting and distributing hateful content to students. The hatred is systemic at UNRWA, and its internal self- auditing mechanisms are not fit for purpose. 3

UNRWA Refused to Take Action, Embarked on Campaign to Smear UN Watch repeatedly urged UNRWA to take action, but they refused. Doctor Wilf claimed that she wrote letters to UNRWA Commissioner General Philippe Lazzarini, and to his predecessor Pierre Krahenbuhl, and requested to meet in order to share information about UNRWA teachers and other staff who support terrorism, but they refused to meet. UN watch affirmed that it was even worse, UNRWA embarked on a strategy to smear our organization for daring to hold them to account.

UN watch continue with another example, "In June 2022, even as UNRWA announced its suspension of six out of 10 UNRWA employees only days after they were exposed by UN Watch for promoting violence and hatred, Deputy Commissioner General Leni Stenseth, a former Norwegian diplomat, donor states that that "the real intent" of UN Watch is "to destroy, not build," and "to invite conflict, not build a lasting peace." She also falsely accused us of "coordinating comments" with "satellite organizations." "

We didn't coordinate the report with anyone, and we have no satellites. Sadly, the U.S. and other Western donor states, who are the stakeholders overseeing UNRWA, apparently made no objections to UNRWA's repeated attacks on our organization.

In another of multiple examples,

UN WATCH New Report, UNRWA's Telegram Group of 3,000 Teachers Celebrating Hamas Massacre of October 7 th

On Friday, the U.S. announced that it was suspending funding to UNRWA over the news that at least a dozen of its employees were implicated in the massacre of October 7 th .

Professor Gur explained that UN WATCH reported that just the day before, however, the State Department had doubled down on its support for UNRWA; it would be allocated a "central" role in post-war Gaza.

saying

UN watch affirmed correctly "Let us be clear: This is a mistake. We call on President Biden to recognize the truth about UNRWA: that it is inimical to the welfare of Palestinians, as well as to the very existence of the State of Israel. "

Doctor Wilf provided a glimpse into the nature of this organization, which employs 13,000 Palestinians in Gaza alone, "in a January 10th that exposed a Telegram chat group of 3,000 UNRWA teachers that is replete with messages, photos and videos celebrating the Hamas massacre of October 7th, mixed with discussions by the educators about when to expect their next UNRWA salaries. "

thread on X

Since then, UN Watch have been diligently working with professional Arabic translators in sifting through more than 249,000 user posts in the chat group.

UN WATCHs come to present their findings, contained in a new report . It documents how UNRWA teachers celebrated the massacre of October 7th, and how they encourage and promote Hamas terrorism.

UNRWA's Terrorgram

Although the position of UNRWA, in the of spokesman Adnan Abu Hasna, is that "we don't know who's in this Telegram group" nor "whether these people work, or don't work for UNRWA," a quick review of the group, user

1   https://unwatch.org/wp-content/uploads/2023/03/ 2023-Report-UNRWA.pdf

2 See UN Watch, UNRWA's Teachers of Hate, June 2022, at 17 . https://unwatch.org/wp- content/uploads/2022/06/2022-Report-UNRWAs-Teachers-of-Hate.pdf 3 https://unwatch.org/un-teacher

11

UNRWA Must Stop Devastating Palestinians and Inciting Racism

Doctor Wilf affirmed that "is time to reform The United Nations Relief and Works Agency for Palestine Refugees in the Near East (UNRWA), an agency whose values are starkly at odds with those of the UN." The UN WATCH described "As set forth in Articles 1 and 2 of the UN Charter, the UN was founded on principles of maintaining international peace and security and promoting friendly relations among nations. However, UNRWA does just the opposite—it spews hatred and exacerbates conflict. "

1. UNRWA perpetuates the Palestinian narrative of the "right of return," whose goal is the elimination of Israel. UNRWA officials openly advocate for the "right of return," as reflected in recent statements, including by UNRWA

Professor Aviv Gur explained "Spokesperson Chris Gunness1 and UNRWA Lebanon director Claudio Cordone,2 that the refugee crisis will continue as

as long as there is no "solution." This "solution" is not resettlement, as it would be for the rest of the world's refugees

handled by the U.N. High Commissioner for Refugees (UNHCR). Unlike UNHCR, UNRWA is not mandated to find durable solutions for the Palestinians.3

As UNRWA expert Einat Wilf has explained, what UNRWA is really giving these Palestinians is the false hope that they will one day be able to return to family homes in Israel abandoned in a war, years before most of them were even born.4

This is obvious from recent statements by UNRWA-registered Palestinians who were born after 1948 and never lived in British Mandatory Palestine or Israel:

Mohammad Afifi, 58-year-old shopkeeper born and raised in Lebanon: "I hold on to UNRWA because I hold on

to my right of returning to Palestine."5

Ramy Mansour, 34-year-old born and raised in Syria: "Take everything and return us to our homes. We don't want any assistance or anything, just return us to our country."6

2. UNRWA's refugee numbers are highly inflated

UNRWA claims it serves five million Palestinian refugees. In fact, only about 20,000 of the original refugees remain. All the rest of the so-called refugees are included because of UNRWA's unique refugee definition which differs

markedly from that of UNHCR. UNHCR defines refugee status according to the Refugee Convention based on a fear of persecution,7 whereas UNRWA's refugee definition is linked purely to residency during the two-year period preceding the 1948 conflict, and also expressly extends to descendants.8

1 Maayan Lubell and Nidal al-Mughrabi, "Schools, health could be hit by U.S. cut for Palestinian refugee funds:

UNRWA chief," Reuters, Jan. 17, 2018.

2 David Enders, "Head of Palestinian relief agency in Lebanon defends works as US threatens to cut funding," The

National, Jan. 11, 2018.

3 Lance Bartholomeusz, "The Mandate of UNRWA at Sixty," Refugee Survey Quarterly, Vol. 28, Nos. 2 & 3, 2010,

p. 471.

4 Haviv Rettig Gur, "Taking refugees off the table," Times of Israel, March 13, 2013.

5 Alexandra Zavis, Noga Tranpolsky and Rushdi Abu Alouf, "In Palestinian territories – and in Israel – jitters over

Trump's threat to cut aid to Palestinians," LA Times, Jan. 7, 2018.

6 Fares Akram, "Across the Mideast, Palestinians brace for Trump aid cuts," Times of Israel, Jan. 16, 2018.

7 1951 Refugee Convention, Article 1.

8 https://www.unrwa.org/palestine-refugees.

In addition, UNRWA stubbornly refuses to find permanent solutions for its refugees, claiming this is not within its mandate. Thus, the anomaly that two million Palestinian "refugees" holding Jordanian citizenship, who UNHCR long

ago would have been removed from its rosters, and continue to be treated by UNRWA as refugees. Similarly, over 2.1 million so called refugees in the West Bank and Gaza enjoy exactly the same rights and privileges as non-refugee Palestinians there.9

Furthermore, there are serious questions as to the accuracy of UNRWA's refugee count, as noted by UNRWA's former

General Counsel James Lindsay and others.10 The recent Lebanese government census which found only 175,000 Palestine refugees in the country,11 by contrast to UNRWA's claim of 450,00012 is a case in point. The UN's own audits criticize UNRWA's deficient oversight.13

3. UNRWA's curriculum and educational staff promote conflict and antisemitism

Education comprises more than half of UNRWA's budget (54%).14 Yet a study published in September 2017 found that

UNRWA textbooks promote conflict, not peace.15 Textbooks claim Jews have no rights in Palestine, deny the existence of Jewish holy places there, and delete Israel from the map. They also promote violent struggle as the path to liberation. Unless change comes from the outside, the curriculum will not be changed any time soon. Following an April 2017 falling-out between UNRWA and the Palestinian Authority (PA) over proposed curriculum changes, UNRWA Commissioner-General Pierre Krähenbühl emphasized that "UNRWA is completely committed to the Palestinian curricula, and that no change will be made..."16 In November 2017, the PA Ministry of Education reiterated its opposition to any attempt by UNRWA to change the curriculum in a way that would contradict the philosophy of the

PA with respect to Palestinian national identity and heritage, i.e., the belief that Jews have no rights in the occupied Palestinian territories and that Palestinians will one day return.17

Inflammatory textbooks aren't the only problem with UNRWA education. UN Watch published detailed reports

in February and April 2017,18 exposing 60 new examples of UNRWA educational staff preaching anti-Semitism and jihadi terrorism to their impressionable students.

Even that is difficult to believe and specially because it is supposed to be a serious and fair international organization the truth is UNRWA is indeed a terrorist promoting body. That in his typical fashion, rather than tackling the issue head-on by firing the antisemitic and terrorist supporting teachers, UNRWA provided them training in what not to post on social media and how to keep social media profiles

"private" so that inflammatory social media posts are not publicly viewable.19 Significantly, UNRWA has never expressed concern about the core underlying problem of students being exposed to anti-Semitism and jihadi terrorism.

Aside from violating the most basic principles of the U.N. charter noted above, such partisanship breeches UNRWA's

neutrality as a UN humanitarian agency, and contravenes Article 29 of the Convention on the Rights of the Child.

9 James G. Lindsay, "Reforming UNRWA," Middle East Quarterly, pp. 85-91, Fall 2012, p. 89.

10 Id., pp. 87-88; Pierre Rehov, "UNRWA: The UN Agency that Creates Palestinian Refugees," Gatestone Institute,

Jan. 29, 2018.

11 "Census finds 174,422 Palestinian refugees in Lebanon," The Daily Star Lebanon, Dec. 21, 2017.

12 https://www.unrwa.org/where-we-work/lebanon.

13 E/AC.51/2017/3, OIOS Audit of UNRWA 2016-17, ¶¶ 53, 57; OIOS Audit of UNRWA 2010, ¶¶ 37-38.

14   https://www.unrwa.org/how-you-can-help/ how-we-spend-funds.

15 Dr. Arnon Grois and DR. Ronni Shaked, "Schoolbooks of the Palestinian Authority (PA): The Attitude to the

Jews, to Israel and to Peace," Simon Wiesenthal Center and Middle East Forum, Sep. 2017.

16 "UNRWA Commissioner-General emphasizes that "UNRWA is completely committed to the Palestinian

curricula and that no change will be made in these curricula," Palestinian Media Watch, April 17,

2017.

17 "PA Ministry of Education strongly opposes any attempt by UNRWA to change the PA curriculum and

schoolbooks," Palestinian Media Watch, Nov. 8, 2017.

18 "Poisoning Palestinian Children," UN Watch, Feb. 2, 2017; "Canada & UNRWA: Enhanced Due Diligence?," UN

Watch, April 10, 2017.

19 "Social media and neutrality training for managers & supervisors

4. UNRWA is a partisan entity with close ties to Hamas

A recent UN audit found that UNRWA was particularly vulnerable to "misappropriation, graft and corruption" in its "procurement, partner selection, food and cash distribution, hiring and promotions, and other areas."20 The audit

expressly criticized the lack of "periodic, unannounced direct inspections of UNRWA shelters and facilities, food distribution centers, schools, and clinics." Unfortunately, this is not surprising given UNRWA's close connections to

Hamas in Gaza.

In June and October 2017, Hamas terror tunnels were discovered under UNRWA schools in Gaza.21

In April 2017, UNRWA teacher and Chairman of the UNRWA Employees Union in Gaza Suhail al-Hindi resigned amid allegations he had been elected to the Hamas leadership. Other UNRWA employee also have been linked to Hamas.22

During the summer 2014 Gaza war, terrorist rockets were stored on, and likely fired from, the premises of UNRWA schools, according to a UN report.23

Each UNRWA school has a Hamas-appointed representative to recruit students to the Islamic Bloc, Hamas's

student group, according to a 2015 report.24

The 2013 documentary "Camp Jihad" shows Palestinian children being indoctrinated to hate Jews and Israel and support martyrdom at an UNRWA summer camp.25

UNRWA employees have exploited their UNRWA privileges to assist terrorist groups like Hamas for years, including by using UNRWA vehicles to transport weapons and terrorists for attacks against Israel.26

If the Human Rights Council is interested in advancing Israeli-Palestinian peace, it should join the call for reforming UNRWA.

20 OIOS Audit of UNRWA 2010, ¶¶ 37-38.

21 "Israel's UN envoy blasts discovery of Gaza tunnel under UNRWA school," Times of Israel, Oct. 29, 2017.

22 "UNRWA's Gaza union head, accused of Hamas ties, no longer employed by agency," Times of Israel, April 23, 2017.

23 "UN admits Palestinians fired rockets from UNRWA schools," UN Watch, April 7, 2015.

24 Paul Alster, "On 65th Anniversary, Looking at UNRWA and its Hamas Ties," The Algemeiner, June 12, 2015.

25 Paul Alster, "U.S. tax dollars help fund UN 'hate camp' in Gaza: documentary," Fox News, Aug. 24, 2013.

26 Asaf Romirowsky, "How UNRWA Support

The Islamo-Leftist Alliance: Threatening Jews and the US

Adam Milstein[32] wrote about this risky and dangerous alliance, the fascist left with the islamic extreme.

Milstein discusses the issue and makes it clear that in the rapidly shifting geopolitical landscape of the 21st century, a disturbing alliance has emerged that poses a profound threat not only to Jews but to Americans and Western civilization as a whole. He describes this alliance, often referred to as the "Islamo-leftist alliance," is a confluence of radical Islamic ideologies and extreme leftist orthodoxy that is united by a 'shared animosity toward Israel, Jews, and the values underpinning Western democracy.'`

Even though there are many different incumbents, "one of the key players in this alliance is the Palestinian wing of the global Muslim Brotherhood, which has been responsible for numerous acts of violence and terrorism against Israelis." affirmed Milstein .

On October 7, this group murdered 1,300 Israelis in a brutal and senseless attack. Since then, Milstein remarks that among others ,"American leftists have shown their support for this extremist group by wearing keffiyehs, setting up encampments across American universities, and openly endorsing the murder of Jews.

The alliance between radical Islamists and extreme leftists is a paradoxical yet potent coalition that is gaining strength and influence in the global political landscape. This alliance uses platforms such as the pulpit in Tehran to condemn the "Zionist regime" and the bullhorn to shout "*** the Police" across American cities. By joining forces, these two groups are able to amplify their message of hate and intolerance, spreading their toxic ideology to a wider audience.

It is crucial for all who value freedom, democracy, and human rights to understand the threat posed by the Islamo-leftist alliance. This alliance seeks to undermine the values and principles that underpin Western civilization, including tolerance, diversity, and respect for

---

32.   https://www.jewishpolicycenter.org/authors/adam-milstein/

human rights. By working together, radical Islamists and extreme leftists are able to advance their agenda of hatred and violence, posing a serious threat to Jews, Americans, and all those who cherish the ideals of democracy and freedom.

In order to combat this dangerous alliance, it is essential for individuals and governments to stand up against extremism and intolerance in all its forms. Holstein advocacy for dialogue, understanding, and cooperation, on his wards ``we can work together to counter the toxic ideology of the Islamo-leftist alliance and uphold the values that are essential to a free and democratic society." Only by standing together against hate and intolerance can we ensure a future where all people are able to live in peace and security, regardless of their religion, ethnicity, or political beliefs.

The Genesis of the Alliance

The origins of the Islamo-leftist alliance can be traced back to a convergence of mutual interests and ideological blind spots. On one side, radical Islamic groups advocate for a fundamentalist worldview that seeks to impose their interpretation of Sharia law in the West and oppose Western influence in the Muslim world. On the other side, extreme leftists push for radical social and political revolution, often viewing Western capitalism as the primary source of global injustice.

Despite their seemingly disparate ideologies, these two groups find common ground in their shared opposition to Western hegemony and perceived injustices. Radical Islamic groups, such as ISIS and Al-Qaeda, see Western intervention in the Muslim world as a form of imperialism and seek to resist and overthrow it. They view the West as a corrupting force that threatens their traditional values and way of life. Similarly, extreme leftists see Western capitalism as exploitative and oppressive, leading to economic inequality and social injustice on a global scale. They believe that dismantling capitalist systems is necessary to achieve social and economic equality.

The Islamo-leftist alliance is also fueled by a sense of victimhood and a desire for empowerment. Both groups see themselves as marginalized and oppressed by Western powers and seek to challenge and disrupt the status quo. By joining forces, they believe they can amplify their voices and increase their influence in the fight against perceived injustices.

However, the alliance between radical Islamic groups and extreme leftists is not without its contradictions and tensions. While they may share common enemies, such as Western imperialism and capitalism, they also have divergent goals and values. Radical Islamic groups often espouse conservative and traditionalist beliefs, including strict adherence to Sharia law and the subjugation of women. On the other hand, extreme leftists advocate for progressive and liberal values, such as gender equality and LGBTQ rights. These ideological differences can create friction within the alliance and lead to conflicts over priorities and strategies.

Furthermore, the Islamo-leftist alliance is not without its critics, who argue that it is based on a flawed and dangerous partnership. Some fear that the alliance could inadvertently legitimize and empower extremist ideologies, leading to increased radicalization and violence. Others worry that it could undermine the principles of secularism and democracy, which are essential for a free and open society.

In conclusion, the origins of the Islamo-leftist alliance can be traced back to a convergence of mutual interests and ideological blind spots. While both groups share a common opposition to Western hegemony and perceived injustices, they also have divergent goals and values that can create tensions within the alliance. It is important to critically examine the implications of this alliance and consider the potential risks and consequences of aligning with groups that may not share the same principles and values.And th

their shared animosity towards the West and its allies. The Islamo-leftist alliance harbors a particular disdain for Israel, the Jewish people, and p their Western values in the Middle East. In the United States, key actors such as the Occupy Movement, Black Lives Matter, Antifa, and the BDS movement align themselves with leftist activists and radical Islamists in Iran and across the Middle East to advance their anti-Western agenda."

This alliance is characterized by a shared language, tactics, and rhetoric aimed at delegitimizing, demonizing, and defaming Israel and the United States. The movement consistently engages in blatant antisemitism, targeting Jews globally and fostering an environment of anti-American hatred and intolerance. By uniting in their hatred towards a common enemy, the Islamo-leftist alliance poses a significant threat to peace and stability in the Middle East and beyond.

Milstein remarks that Islamo-leftist alliance is a dangerous coalition that is fueled by a mutual hatred towards the West and its allies. By joining forces, radical Islamic groups and extreme leftists are able to amplify their anti-Western rhetoric and advance their shared agenda of undermining Western values and institutions. It is imperative that we recognize and confront the dangers posed by this alliance in order to safeguard peace and security in the Middle East and around the world.

The Threat to Jewish Communities

In recent years, there has been a concerning rise in anti-Semitism around the world, with Jewish communities facing severe and alarming implications as a result of the alliance between Islamists and fascist leftists. This alliance has sought to normalize anti-Semitic discourse under the guise of political criticism, using the label of "anti-Zionism" to disguise their true intentions. As a result, Jews are increasingly being excluded from communal spaces, organizations, and institutions, effectively marginalizing them within society.

The renowned philanthropist and community leader, Adam Milstein, has been vocal about the dangers posed by this Islamo-leftist alliance and its impact on Jewish communities worldwide. He has highlighted how anti-Semitism, with its long and dark history, has resurged with intensity in recent years, fueled by the rhetoric and actions of this alliance. By rebranding anti-Semitism as anti-Zionism, they have been able to cloak their hateful views in a veneer of political legitimacy, making it more socially acceptable to espouse anti-Semitic beliefs.

One of the key tactics employed by the Islamo-leftist alliance is to use the question "Are you a Zionist?" as a litmus test for entry into leftist circles. By framing support for Israel as synonymous with support for oppression and colonialism, they seek to alienate and ostracize Jews who identify as Zionists. This tactic effectively serves to exclude Jews from leftist spaces, where they may otherwise find common cause on issues such as social justice and human rights.

The ultimate goal of this tactic is to marginalize Jews within society, denying them a voice and a place at the table in discussions about important issues. By painting all Jews as supporters of the right wing the Islamo-leftist alliance seeks to delegitimize Jewish voices and perspectives, effectively silencing them in public discourse. This exclusion not only harms Jewish individuals, but also weakens the fabric of society as a whole, depriving us of the diversity of thought and experience that is essential for a thriving democracy.

It is crucial to push back against this insidious form of anti-Semitism disguised as political criticism. We all must stand in solidarity with Jewish communities around the world, affirming their right to exist and participate fully in society without fear of discrimination or marginalization. By challenging the normalization of anti-Semitic discourse and rejecting the exclusionary tactics of the Islamo-leftist alliance, we can work towards a more inclusive and just society for all.

Adam Milstein correctly warns that the consequences of this wave of modern antisemitism go beyond just physical safety, as it also seeks to undermine the historical and cultural identity of Jews. The delegitimization of Israel, a core tactic of the Islamo-leftist agenda, aims to sever the connection between Jews and their ancestral homeland. While the Muslim world has long attempted to delegitimize Israel, leftist leaders in countries such as South Africa, Ireland, Spain, and Norway have now taken up this cause. This delegitimization not only affects Jews in Israel but also creates fear and insecurity within Jewish communities worldwide.

The irresponsible and definitely perverse refusal of leftist leaders to associate with and legitimize the Jewish state is not only politically motivated but also puts Jewish communities at risk.Milstein remarks `` By appeasing the will of antisemitic activists, these leaders are contributing to the rise of antisemitism and putting more Jews in danger. "

It's a fact that targeting Jewish students on college campuses, as well as the increasing number of hate crimes against synagogues and Jewish institutions, is a direct result of this alliance between Islamists and leftists.

There are complicated and dangerous consequences of this evil alliance. And as Milstein explained "the implications of the alliance between Islamists and leftists for Jewish communities worldwide are severe and far-reaching. The normalization of antisemitic discourse under the guise of "anti-Zionism" not only endangers the physical safety of Jews but also seeks to undermine their historical and cultural identity."

Facing the complex reality "It is imperative that we recognize and condemn this wave of modern antisemitism and work towards creating a society where all individuals, regardless of their religious or cultural background, can feel safe and secure."

The Broader Threat to America

It's dangerous and definitely irresponsable to try to skip the reality , indeed the threat that the Islamo-leftist alliance poses is significant to America and its foundational values, beyond just targeting Jews.

Indeed this coalition seeks to dismantle the principles of democracy, freedom, individual liberty, and pluralism that define Western civilization,and specially the USA.

Their hatredtowards Israel and the Jewish people is intertwined with their rejection of American exceptionalism and America's international power.

It is not a coincidence that every "pro-Hamas" march and rally, often disguised as "Pro-Palestinian," is filled with antisemitic imagery and rhetoric, as well as anti-American sentiment. American flags are burned alongside Israeli flags, and calls for the destruction of Israel are followed by anti-American chants. This alliance not only targets Israel and the Jewish community but also threatens American civil liberties, values, and freedoms.

One of the main important ways in which this alliance poses a threat to America is through its frontal attack on democracy and freedom.

Democracy is a fundamental and basic principle of Western civilization, allowing for the peaceful transfer of power and the protection of individual rights. The Islamo-leftist alliance seeks to undermine democracy by promoting authoritarian regimes and ideologies that suppress dissent and limit freedom of speech.

Furthermore, the alliance poses a threat to individual liberty. The principles of individual liberty, such as freedom of speech, religion, and assembly, are essential to the American way of life. The Islamo-leftist alliance seeks to restrict these freedoms by promoting censorship and silencing dissenting voices. This not only threatens the rights of individuals but also undermines the democratic process.

Pluralism, another foundational value of Western civilization, is also under attack by the Islamo-leftist alliance. Pluralism celebrates diversity and tolerance, allowing for different beliefs and perspectives to coexist peacefully. The alliance seeks to impose a singular ideology and suppress dissenting views, leading to a homogenized society that stifles creativity and innovation.

The Islamo-leftist alliance poses a broader threat to America and its foundational values beyond just targeting Jews. By seeking to dismantle democracy, individual liberty, and pluralism, this coalition undermines the principles that define Western civilization. It is essential for Americans to recognize and resist this threat in order to protect their freedoms and values.

1. Undermining Institutions: The extreme fascist intolerant left and radical Islamists disdain the foundational values underpinning Western civilization. Together, they promote a narrative-based view of history, avoiding fact-based objective analysis. This can be best seen across American academia, where ideological views are given priority over academic integrity and the pursuit of truth. The same leftist worldview, and the commitment to a stringent Marxist political orthodoxy, has also taken over American corporations and much of the media. The recent leftist obsession with demonizing the police perfectly encapsulates the Islamo-fascist leftist overlap. The Black Lives Matter movement and associated protests maintain a posture that's anti-police and anti-Israel. Furthering this connection, both radical Islamists and leftists disseminate propaganda that connects Israel to American policing practices and training.

Milstein describes correctly that "The extreme left and radical Islamists share a common disdain for the foundational values that underpin Western civilization. Both groups promote a narrative-based view of history, avoiding fact-based objective analysis in favor of pushing their own ideological agendas. This can be seen most prominently in American academia, where ideological views are often given priority over academic integrity and the pursuit of truth.

The increasingly lost fascist leftist worldview, along with the progressive central left, has been captured by antisemitic leaders who adhere to a stringent Marxist political orthodoxy. This ideology has infiltrated American corporations and much of the media, leading to a situation where ideological purity is valued over objective reporting and analysis. While the language of individuals like Mr. Milstein may sound politically incorrect, it is important to acknowledge the truth behind his words.

The failure of each Marxist experiment throughout history serves as a reminder of the destructive nature of communist parties. These parties often contribute to frustration, pain, controversies, and instability in the countries they govern. The recent leftist obsession with demonizing the police is a prime example of this trend. The Black Lives Matter movement and associated protests maintain an anti-police stance, often drawing connections between law enforcement and systemic racism.

It is crucial to recognize the dangers of allowing ideological purity to overshadow critical thinking and rational discourse. When individuals and organizations prioritize adherence to a specific political orthodoxy over objective analysis, the result is often a distorted view of reality. This can lead to the spread of misinformation, the suppression of dissenting voices, and the erosion of democratic principles.

In order to combat this trend, it is essential for individuals to engage in open and honest dialogue, to challenge prevailing narratives, and to seek out diverse perspectives. By fostering a culture of intellectual curiosity and critical thinking, we can work towards a more informed and inclusive society. It is only through a commitment to truth and reason that we can hope to overcome the divisive forces that threaten to tear us apart.

American policing practices and the Israeli government's treatment of Palestinians.

The overlap between radical Islamists and the extreme left is a concerning trend that has become increasingly evident in recent years. One of the key ways in which these two groups align is through their shared propaganda efforts. Both groups disseminate misinformation that connects Israel to American policing practices and training, furthering their anti-Israel and anti-police narratives. This propaganda serves to demonize both Israel and law enforcement agencies, painting them as oppressive forces that must be resisted.

The propaganda efforts of radical Islamists and the extreme left often focus on drawing parallels between the actions of Israel and those of American police forces. By linking these two entities, both groups are able to further their anti-Israel and anti-police narratives. This propaganda often takes the form of misinformation and exaggeration, with the goal of inciting anger and resentment towards both Israel and law enforcement agencies.

In academia, this narrative-based approach to history and current events has led to a distortion of the truth. Students are often taught a skewed version of history that aligns with the ideological views of their professors, rather than being presented with a balanced and fact-based analysis. This has serious implications for the future of education and intellectual discourse, as students are not being equipped with the critical thinking skills necessary to deal with complexity.

The overlap between radical Islamists and the extreme left in their propaganda efforts is a dangerous trend that must be addressed. By disseminating misinformation that connects Israel to American policing practices and training, both groups are able to further their anti-Israel and anti-police narratives. This propaganda serves to demonize both Israel and law enforcement agencies, painting them as oppressive forces that must be resisted.

The overlap between radical Islamists and the extreme left in their propaganda efforts is a concerning trend that has serious implications for education and intellectual discourse. By disseminating misinformation that connects Israel to American policing practices and training, both groups are able to further their anti-Israel and anti-police narratives. It is important for individuals to critically evaluate the information they are presented with and to seek out balanced and fact-based analysis in order to combat this dangerous trend.

engage with complex issues in a nuanced and informed manner.

In conclusion, the extreme left and radical Islamists share a common disdain for the foundational values of Western civilization. Their promotion of a narrative-based view of history, which prioritizes ideology over objective analysis, has had a detrimental impact on American academia, corporations, and media. It is essential that we push back against this trend and uphold the principles of academic integrity and the pursuit of truth in all areas of society.q

2. Erosion of Free Speech and Expression: A key component of the Islamo-leftist strategy is to silence dissent through social and political pressure. Radical leftists often employ "cancel culture" to stifle voices that challenge their orthodoxy, while Islamists use accusations of Islamophobia to suppress criticism of extremist ideologies. Leftists also increasingly look to compel speech, mandating terminology to limit freedom of expression. Land acknowledgements, mandatory pronouns, and disclaimers are all arrows in the leftist quiver. Anyone who refuses to comply with their speech code faces discrimination and ostracization. This assault on freedom of speech and freedom of expression threatens the open discourse essential to a functioning democracy.

3. The Rigid Adoption of Identity Politics: Both groups exploit identity politics to fracture society along strictly defined racial, religious, and ideological lines. By emphasizing group identity over individual merit, they create an environment ripe for conflict and division. American corporations and the public school system obsess

over DEI policies, Critical Race Theory (CRT), and intersectionality. These ideological movements threaten American prosperity and cohesion. Additionally, meritocracy, a fundamental component of the American capitalist system, is verboten in leftist circles. Meritocracy has a proven track record of transcending identity and is often the most useful tool for economic advancement. Despite its value, leftists view meritocracy as a fundamentally racist concept and eagerly seek its demise. This poses a grave threat to the American economic, educational, and political future.

4. Support for Extremist Groups: The Islamo-leftist alliance operating model relies on international reciprocity. Domestic leftist groups and international Islamic groups offer tacit political cover and explicit financial funding to one another. Leftist groups adhere to critical theory and simplify every interaction based on power dynamics, where there's an "oppressor" and an "oppressed." This is why they sympathize with terrorist organizations such as Hamas and Hezbollah (the "oppressed"). Their continued anti-Israel activism in the West validates terrorism in the Middle East. Concurrently, anti-Israel groups like Students for Justice in Palestine, Jewish Voice for Peace, and Codepink receive direct funding from anti-American entities around the globe including Qatar, China, Russia, and Iran. America's enemies effectively weaponize these groups as influence campaigns to sow division in America from within. The Islamo-leftist global alignment not only endangers lives but also destabilizes regions crucial to global security.

The Global Implications

The principle of free speech is a cornerstone of American democracy, allowing for the open exchange of ideas and the robust debate necessary for a healthy society. Upholding this principle is essential to ensuring that all voices are heard, even those that may be unpopular or controversial. Without the protection of free speech, dissenting opinions can be silenced, and the marketplace of ideas can be stifled.

In recent years, there has been a growing trend towards silencing dissenting voices and imposing restrictions on free speech. This trend is dangerous, as it undermines the very foundation of democracy and threatens the rights and freedoms of all citizens. Compelled speech, where individuals are forced to express certain views or opinions against their will, is particularly concerning as it infringes on the fundamental right to freedom of expression.

One of the key arguments in favor of free speech is that it allows for the marketplace of ideas to flourish. When individuals are free to express their opinions, no matter how controversial or unpopular, it allows for a diversity of perspectives to be heard. This diversity is essential for a healthy democracy, as it ensures that all viewpoints are considered and debated. By silencing dissenting voices, we risk creating an echo chamber where only certain ideas are allowed to be expressed, leading to a narrowing of public discourse.

Furthermore, free speech is essential for holding those in power accountable. Without the ability to criticize and challenge authority, there is a risk of government overreach and abuse of power. The ability to speak out against injustice and corruption is a fundamental right that must be protected in order to maintain a functioning democracy.

However, there are those who argue that certain forms of speech, such as hate speech or speech that incites violence, should be restricted in the name of protecting marginalized groups. While it is important to condemn and combat hate speech, it is also important to recognize that censorship is not the answer. Instead, we must rely on counter-speech and education to combat harmful ideas, while still upholding the principle of free speech.

In conclusion, the principle of free speech is essential for a healthy democracy. It allows for the open exchange of ideas, the robust debate necessary for progress, and the ability to hold those in power accountable. While there may be calls to restrict certain forms of speech, it is important to remember that the protection of free speech is vital to ensuring that all voices are heard and that democracy thrives. We must continue to uphold this principle, even in the face of challenges, in order to protect our rights and freedoms as citizens.

To combat this trend, it is crucial to reaffirm our commitment to free speech and resist efforts to censor or suppress differing viewpoints. This requires a staunch dedication to protecting the right to criticize and debate ideas without fear of retribution. It also means standing up against compelled speech and ensuring that individuals are free to express their own beliefs without coercion.

In addition to upholding the principle of free speech, it is important to build and maintain strong alliances with other democracies and moderate Muslim-majority nations. These alliances are essential in countering the spread of radical ideologies and promoting peace, security, and economic opportunity. Initiatives such as the Abraham Accords have shown the power of collaboration in advancing shared goals and values.

Supporting Israel is also crucial in the fight against radical Islam and in upholding democratic values. Israel serves as a frontline state in the battle against extremism and is a key ally in promoting peace and cooperation in the Middle East. Efforts to delegitimize and demonize Israel, such as the BDS movement, must be opposed, and initiatives that promote peace and stability in the region should be supported.

Defending liberalism and combating radical leftist ideologies are also important in preserving the values that have made America a beacon of freedom and prosperity. Leaders must make a strong case for the benefits of American liberal values, including First Amendment rights, multiculturalism, and capitalism. By promoting these values with confidence and conviction, we can counter the efforts of the Islamo-leftist alliance to undermine Western culture and unity.

In conclusion, the Islamo-leftist alliance poses a significant threat to the values and principles that define Western civilization. By reaffirming our commitment to free speech, strengthening alliances, supporting Israel, defending liberalism, and countering extremism, we can confront this threat and safeguard the future of the West. It is imperative that we stand united in defense of liberty, justice, and democracy for all.

PA Official: Palestinians Approve Paying Terrorists More Than Civil Servants, support and incentivize terrorism.

Professors Itamar Marcus and Ephraim D. Tepler have been at the forefront of exposing the true colors of the Palestinian public opinion and the real sentiment of the Palestinian Authority. Through their research and publications, they have shed light on the disturbing reality of the Palestinian leadership's support for terrorism and violence.

Professor Itamar Marcus is the founder and director of Palestinian Media Watch, an organization dedicated to monitoring and analyzing the Palestinian media and education systems. Professor Marcus has been instrumental in uncovering the glorification of terrorism and incitement to violence in Palestinian society. His research has revealed how the Palestinian Authority routinely honors and rewards terrorists, portraying them as heroes and martyrs.

Professor Ephraim D. Tepler is a renowned expert on Middle Eastern politics and has conducted extensive research on the Palestinian Authority's policies and actions. He has highlighted the Palestinian leadership's double standards when it comes to condemning terrorism. While publicly denouncing terrorism to the international community, the Palestinian Authority continues to financially support and incentivize terrorists and their families.

Together, Professors Marcus and Tepler have exposed the hypocrisy and deception of the Palestinian leadership. Their work has challenged the prevailing narrative that the . Instead, they have revealed the true nature of the Palestinian leadership as supporters of terrorism and violence.

The recent decision by the Palestinian Authority to pay salaries to terrorists and their families is a stark reminder of the dangerous ideology that permeates Palestinian society. It is a clear indication that the Palestinian leadership prioritizes violence and terrorism over peace and coexistence. Professors Marcus and Tepler's research has provided valuable insights into the mindset of the Palestinian leadership and the challenges that lie ahead in achieving a lasting peace in the region.

In conclusion, Professors Itamar Marcus and Ephraim D. Tepler have been instrumental in exposing the true colors of the Palestinian public opinion and the real sentiment of the Palestinian Authority. Their research and publications have provided valuable insights into the dangerous ideology that drives the Palestinian leadership and the obstacles to peace in the region. It is essential to continue supporting and amplifying their work in order to challenge the prevailing narratives and work towards a more peaceful and just future for all.

. Obviously the West, the USA officials and the progressive camp and certainly the left militant will express they understanding to this evil decision

Even more important the Israeli left and the socialist international organization and even the social democratic parties will argue that those are desperate actions provoked by the "occupation" and again the West choice will be not to hear that the Palestinian leaders are expression and instead to "interpretare" a soft and friendly version.

The same happens when the worldwide slogan " from the river to the sea ". Its true that the majority of them doesn't know which river and neither wich sea, but those who know ,are expressing they wish to sent the jews to the sea and to annihilate the Jewish people and the Jewish state

The Palestinian Authority (PA) is going through a major financial crisis and cannot afford to pay its employees their full salaries.

Nonetheless, according to a PA official, Palestinian civil servants are happy that the PA prioritizes paying terrorists in prison 100% of their terror reward salaries, while the civil servants themselves receive only 50% of their monthly salary (though today, they claim the salaries are equal).

Muhammad Hamida, Economy Ministry Director in Bethlehem: "While we as [public] employees received a salary at a rate of 50%, before the [Gaza] war, the families of the prisoners and Martyrs [i.e., terrorists] received a full salary. The Palestinian leadership remains committed to this. It deducted amounts from regular employees and gave a full salary to the families of the prisoners and Martyrs.

Today, everyone is equal. The salaries that the families of the Martyrs and prisoners receive are also received by the employees. We are proud of the prisoners and their families as well as of the Martyrs and their families. .. This is a national question, a very important one, and it is a priority. No one in Palestine complains about why the families of the prisoners and the Martyrs get full salary and we get half." [emphasis added]

[Official PA TV, July 16, 2024]

Professor Aviv explained that this shows how well the Palestinian Authority has succeeded in brainwashing its population to believe that terrorists deserve more money than Palestinian government employees, even though they do not work and have no expenses.

PA TV has broadcast PA President Mahmoud Abbas' well-known proclamation dozens of times that even "if the PA has one penny left[33], it will continue to pay prisoners and Martyrs before anyone else."

Another PA official recently stressed yet again that terrorists should be paid before all other Palestinians:

Effectively Jordan Valley District Governor Hussein Hamayel express : "When great pressures were exerted on [PA] President Mahmoud Abbas and the Palestinian leadership to stop the salaries () of the Martyrs and the prisoners [i.e., terrorists], or to create tools to pay them so that they would constitute a prelude to stopping the salaries and allowances of the prisoners and the Martyrs, the president's position was clear and it represents all the Palestinians by him saying:

33.　　https://palwatch.org/page/35238

'If one penny is left in our pockets, it will be paid to the prisoners and the Martyrs.'

And he added that "This is something strategic for us, something that is not subject to any issue connected to pressures, extortion, blockade, or threats from here or there. This is a clear position for us that we will continue."

[Fatah Commission of Information and Culture, Facebook page, April 17, 2024]

Palestinian Media Watch[34] that is doing a very professional work has exposed for years that the PA leadership sees its Martyrs and prisoners as the most important and honored people in society who deserve more financial rewards than people who work.

It could sound insane and maybe unbelievable but it is the truth.

The problem is that the western usually doesn't want to hear that the Palestinian are saying .In fact is the same when most of the westerners, especially in the progressive camp affirm without any proof that Hamas terrorists group doesn't represent the Palestinians, indeed there are many pools that shows sadly the opposite, the terrorist organization is the admired by a vast majority of Palestinians, and most of them are proud about the massacre of jews in October 2023.

So it's absolutely logical and expected that

PA officials are stressing that glorifying and rewarding terrorists is supported by the entire Palestinian population.

Doctor Wilf remarks that legal actions worldwide against UNRWA for complicity with terrorism have gained momentum in recent years, with victims seeking justice and accountability for the agency's ties to terrorist organizations. From lawsuits in Canada to complaints in France, individuals and organizations are taking action to hold UNRWA responsible for its alleged support of terrorism.

Inat Wilf explained that in Canada, a lawsuit has been filed against the Government of Canada for renewing funding for UNRWA despite

---

34.   http://palwatch.org/

documented links between the agency and Hamas. The lawsuit argues that this decision violates Canadian law and seeks judicial review of the government's actions. Additionally, in the United States, civil damages lawsuits have been brought against UNRWA and its senior officials by victims of a Hamas massacre. These lawsuits allege that UNRWA intentionally facilitated funding to Hamas, leading to further terrorist activities.

Furthermore, in the United States, a lawsuit has been filed to stop government funding to UNRWA until the agency can prove that none of its funds are being diverted to terrorist activities. This lawsuit, brought by over 8,000 Israeli and American citizens, seeks to hold the U.S. government accountable for its support of UNRWA. In France, complaints have been made to government officials regarding the financing of UNRWA, citing the agency's complicity with terrorism as a violation of French law.

These legal actions are really important and highlight the growing concern over UNRWA's alleged ties to terrorist organizations and the need for accountability and transparency within the agency.

It's possible that this will be first step of .any in order to restore some logics and justice in the long and bloody middle east conflicts

By taking legal action against UNRWA, victims and advocates are seeking to ensure that the agency is held responsible for any support it may provide to terrorist groups. As these cases progress, it will be important to monitor the outcomes and implications for UNRWA's operations and funding.